RHODODENDRONS

ACKNOWLEDGEMENTS

I wish to express my thanks to Mr Peter Cox of Glendoick, Perthshire, for his considerable help in allowing me to reprint the international list of nurseries and societies from his book *The Smaller Rhododendrons* and for providing additional up-to-date information.

Also to my secretary, Annette Pascual, for her work in typing the manuscript and her ability to decipher my hieroglyphics which pass as handwriting.

SERIES EDITOR · VINCENT PAGE

RHODODENDRONS

John Street

Photographs by Vincent Page

CASSELL

Cassell Publishers Limited
Villiers House, 41/47 Strand
London WC2N 5JE

First paperback edition 1990
First published in 1987 by Century Hutchinson Ltd

British Library Cataloguing in Publication Data
Street, John *1917–*
Rhododendrons.
1. Gardens. Rhododendrons
I. Title
635.93362

ISBN 0-304-34008-1

Illustrations by Vana Haggerty

Original edition designed and produced by
Justin Knowles Publishing Group
Exeter

Typeset by Keyspools Ltd
Printed and bound in Hong Kong

Contents

LIST OF PLATES

FOREWORD

My father, Gomer Waterer, had two absorbing interests – one was rhododendrons, the other the game of golf. In the evening the golf news in *The Times* usually held his attention, but one person, John Street, usually had little difficulty in making him put down the paper and turn his talk back to the rhododendrons they both loved.

That was more than fifty years ago. After World War II, I returned to the Knap Hill Nursery while John threw himself enthusiastically into the task of rebuilding his nursery. At the Chelsea Show of 1948 my wife and I gazed with astonishment and admiration at his splendid exhibit: we had never seen rhododendrons shown with greater qualities of flower and foliage.

Soon after the War, John developed the taste for writing that must have been inherent in him. His lucid and colourful style well equipped him to write regularly for *The Horticultural Trade Journal* (now called *Horticulture Week*), and this he has done for many years under the pen-name 'Woodsman'. He has always attended Chelsea before the opening day and approached anyone he thought might provide him with subject matter for his weekly articles.

Rhododendrons, however, have been his first love, and he has helped to bring them to the attention of the public over many years. This book, beautifully illustrated by Vincent Page's photographs, is a valuable addition to John Street's written work. It will be a source of encouragement to all those who are already growing and enjoying rhododendrons and an inspiration to those who have not yet attempted to grow one of these lovely plants in their own gardens.

G. Donald Waterer, May 1987

INTRODUCTION
A PERSONAL
APPRECIATION

While it might seem that as the third generation of a family growing rhododendrons since 1869 I might have had them thrust upon me but this was not so. My forebears grew a wide variety of trees and shrubs, including many rhododendrons, but I came to like them so much that they became almost an obsession, and for the last 25 years I have grown them to the exclusion of all other plants. They are very satisfying to grow commercially, and the end product, even when out of flower, is a beautiful sight. But to grow them well requires skill and considerable expertise. You never stop learning, and it seems that the more you know the more you need to know. Now that I have retired I feel sometimes that I would like to start all over again with the benefit of experience – which is 'the name men give to their mistakes'. That rather sad French proverb *Si jeunesse savait, si vieillesse pouvait* also seems appropriate.

Rhododendrons give pleasure to a great many people and they have been well described as 'good garden decorators' but they have less obvious charms. They always hold a promise of flower to come in the big buds that set late in the summer and are carried through the winter. Not only that but they are handsome evergreens in their own right, many of them having distinctive foliage which adds to their charm.

One of the skills of the professional grower is the ability to tell the names of the different varieties by their leaf and habit alone, even when they are out of flower. It takes some years to acquire this knowledge and it is one of those esoteric skills in horticulture which, to the uninitiated, seem to be almost magic. For example, I am always amazed that a rose grower can tell a variety often by simply feeling the thorns while those who grow fruit trees can tell one from the other by the habit and growth. Compared with these two skills, the ability to distinguish one rhododendron from another by the leaves is not so difficult as it would seem at first. A few are very easy: 'Britannia', with its broad leaves in a very light green, almost yellow, colour, is quite different from 'Doncaster', which has narrow pointed leaves and a bushy habit. One or two are difficult: 'Countess of Derby' and 'Professor Hugo de Vries' are almost identical, not only in their leaf and growth but also in the flower, and 'Pink Pearl' and 'Mother of Pearl' are indistinguishable in the leaf but very different in flower, one a relatively deep pink and the other pearly white.

Not only are there many different varieties – at one time I grew as many as 200 in my own nursery – but the same varieties do not always behave in the same way every year. For example, there is often a great difference in the time they flower. This can be particularly unfortunate when it comes to arranging colour schemes. One of the most attractive colour combinations in all flowers is the mixture of yellows and purples in their various forms and tones right down to cream and mauve. This is seen at its best in the varieties 'Goldsworth Yellow' and 'Purple Splendour' which often flower together. Yet sometimes and for no apparent reason, 'Goldsworth Yellow' can be out and over while 'Purple Splendour' is only just showing colour with the buds breaking.

The quality of the flowers varies considerably too from year to year. I amuse myself by awarding an imaginary 'Oscar' to the variety that gave the best performance in any particular season. At times it is difficult to choose between them, but some varieties seem to need particular weather conditions to be at their best. One of the star plants of my second exhibit at the Chelsea Flower Show in 1949 was 'Mrs P.D. Williams', yet thereafter it was never as good again until 1987; it flowered and was attractive in the intervening years, but it lacked that fine quality it had on those two spectacular occasions.

The flowering season and subsequent growing season are times of great pleasure for all rhododendron growers, but there are even greater joys (and disasters) for the professional, most arising from the different stages of propagation.

Here, however, I have to admit to what can only be considered an attitude bordering on a restrictive practice. Much of the fun has gone out of the commercial propagation of rhododendrons now that growing them from cuttings has taken the place of grafting, and my former manager, who was with me for 28 years, aided and abetted me in this reluctance to move on to the more economic and commercially viable system of propagating by cuttings. We were both hesitant to lose our old skills, perhaps forever.

First, there was raising the stocks, hundreds of thousands of *R. ponticum* grown from seed. This was done in a long brick frame with a somewhat complicated compost. Fine sifted leaf mould and peat on top for good and quick germination, and something with a bit more body in it below for better growth once the seed had germinated. About three weeks after sowing would come the first thrill – the sight of that almost imperceptible flush of green, showing that the seeds were just beginning to sprout, which you could see only by putting your head in the frame and looking sideways.

Then we 'thumbed them out', a job that was the speciality of one man who learnt it from his father. Next, we followed their progress through to the time when they were good stocks – 'pencil thickness' was the crucial measurement – to be lifted and laid in peat beds to draw root. This was the next critical time. We liked to start grafting at the end of April, but it would have been useless, only courting disaster, to have begun this task before those stocks were a mass of young white roots. Sometimes we had to delay the main operation until the middle of May which meant that we had a rushed job to finish before the scions had made too much growth.

Then, the grafting itself, a highly skilled job, and the quicker it was done by men who knew what they were doing, the better. There were four of us who could do this, and it became the top priority job for us all throughout May and into June. It was a family affair, rather like hay-making and harvesting on a farm in the old days. We worked from eight in the morning until eight at night. My wife prepared tea for us at five, and it was brought out to us by the children before the overtime session. When the work was finished we celebrated with a party in the garden, inviting everyone who had been involved, including the office staff and the casuals hired to keep the weeds down while we were so fully occupied.

The grafts were planted in frames under double glass, a job that was done for years by one man, even when he was an old age pensioner. Highly skilled at the work, he was an inveterate gambler, and always had Tuesday evening off for the whist drive in the village hall. The grafts would be closed down in the frames, tightly sealed, and not touched for three weeks when, as the manager used to say, we would 'break the magic' by opening them for the first time to look for signs of callus, the 'blisters' of growth that unite the scion to the stock.

Next came the long process of hardening them off throughout the summer. Then, at the end, seeing those frames solid with young grafts with all the variation of foliage of the different varieties was a reward in itself.

Now with cuttings, given the right heat in a greenhouse and rooting auxins, the work can be done by anyone once they have been shown the simple way to make a cutting. All the skill and craftsmanship have gone.

For me, the most exciting part of growing rhododendrons and the one I miss most was preparing and staging an exhibit at the Chelsea Flower Show. It was a long drawn out gamble from September to May. Once the space was booked there was no going back. It definitely had to be 'all right on the night', and when the present Lord Aberconway succeeded his father as President of the Royal Horticultural Society, it had to be 'better than ever', because he always ended his speech at the luncheon for the Press with those words.

It has to be admitted that the groups exhibited at Chelsea are the very best that can be staged by the nurserymen who exhibit at the show. They have to be, even though the financial rewards, in the way of orders for plants, never cover the costs. There is something about Chelsea that brings out the best in both the plants and the people, but it is somewhat ingenuous to pretend that an amateur can achieve the same results.

We would begin our preparations in September, when we would select the very best plants before any were sold – our relatively small exhibit was made up of the pick of some 30,000 plants. These would be lifted, and either put in tubs or pots or their roots would be wrapped in dead bracken held in place with chicken wire. They would be housed under cover for the winter, the late-flowering varieties in a greenhouse and the earlies in a shade house made with builders' laths. The very late varieties, which would need forcing, were left out until they had suffered a slight frost, because they need that stimulus before they can be given any heat to bring them on.

All the time they would need to be watered and fed until they began slowly to expand their buds, which was when the hard work started. They would have to be moved in and out of the different houses, some even into the shade house if they were too far forward, so they would all be perfect for the day – that is, with most of the flower open and just two or three 'pips' still to expand to make the truss complete.

Taking them to the show was fraught with anxiety. Loading them into the lorries was a work of art, again a job for one man who was particularly good at it. Staging the exhibit took two or three days because the regulations were much stricter then – all pots and containers had to be covered with moss, almost as if there was something vulgar about them, rather like the Victorians covering their table legs in case the sight of them might offend the delicate sensibility of the young ladies of the day.

There is nothing quite like the work of preparing for the show. Not only is it a fascinating job – flower arrangement on the grand scale – but the camaraderie among the exhibitors is something beyond even the *esprit de corps* of a good company of soldiers. Everyone is willing to help everyone, and I do believe that if a regular exhibitor had suddenly lost all his plants through some remarkable and unfortunate accident the others would have found enough spares to fill his space.

This spirit was fostered and encouraged – inspired perhaps might be the better word – by the two presidents I knew, the present Lord Aberconway and his father, who were round the show all the time during the days of preparation with words of advice and encouragement. It would not be going too far to say that some of the happiest days of my life were spent preparing for Chelsea. The show, when it opened, was something of an anti-climax. That last look at the final exhibit when it was all finished was enough.

John Street, May 1987

A BRIEF HISTORY

There is little doubt that the rhododendron in its various forms is the most decorative evergreen flowering shrub that can be grown in the open garden in the temperate zone. It has only one limitation – it must have an acid soil, without lime.

And yet, paradoxically, the first rhododendron ever to be grown in England, in 1656, is the only exception to this rule, which probably accounts for it surviving for so long. This is the Alpine Rose (*Rhododendron hirsutum*), which features so often on postcards of Switzerland. Unfortunately, those pictures are somewhat flattering; not so much because the appearance and colour have been enhanced by artful photography, but because when the plant is taken away from its natural habitat to be grown in gardens, it is not quite so attractive. The reason for this is that when it is grown in a softer climate and a richer soil, it is inclined to become lank and unkempt, losing the natural dwarf and bushy habit which it has under the rigorous conditions in the Alps. It grows more satisfactorily in the north of England and in Scotland than it does in the Midlands and the south, but even then it is really only a species that would be grown by an enthusiast with an alkaline soil, who is determined to have a rhododendron of some sort. However, being the one exception to the rule, *R. hirsutum* does serve to emphasize the rhododendron's essential need for an acid soil.

It is not quite clear how *R. hirsutum* came to the United Kingdom. It was first discovered and named by the 16th century Flemish botanist, Charles l'Ecluse, who later adopted the name Clusius. Clusius may have sent it to one of his correspondents, for it is mentioned by John Gerard in his famous *Herbal*. It is known to have been grown by John Tradescant Senior in his garden at Lambeth in London, and it is possible that it may have been brought to England by Huguenot refugees.

The next rhododendron to arrive in the United Kingdom was *R. maximum* in 1736. It was the first from North America and came as the result of the partnership between the Quaker haberdasher, Peter Collinson, and John Bartram, a farmer of Pennsylvania, who took up botany and later was appointed King's botanist in America. Collinson found the finance for Bartram's expeditions in search of plants and attended to the disposal of the specimens he sent home, growing them in his own garden at Mill Hill in London, and selling them to the 'curious gardeners' of the day to provide more funds for further expeditions.

It is doubtful if there are any plants of *R. maximum* now being grown in Britain, because it is not very decorative. One of its faults is that it flowers late, by which time the young shoots have grown so much that the small flowers are almost hidden. Against that, it is very hardy and late flowering.

There are very few recorded hybrids raised from it, but its influence can be seen indirectly in many of those raised in the early part of the 19th century. It is probably responsible for the blotch or spot in the flowers of many hybrids, and several of the rhododendrons raised by the Waterers of Knaphill and Bagshot before 1850 have this characteristic. Probably the most distinct of them all is 'Lady Eleanor Cathcart', raised by John Waterer as a direct cross between *R. maximum* and *R. arboreum*. The story is told in the Bagshot nursery of how the original seedling of this cross, which was selected for naming, was sent away by mistake as an unnamed seedling in a batch of rejects for use in a planting scheme. When the mistake was discovered, the head carter was sent out to bring back the precious seedling under cover of darkness and replace it with another plant from the same batch, but one that had not been selected for naming.

R. ponticum was first discovered in Spain between Cadiz and Gibraltar by Claes Alstroemer, a pupil of Linnaeus, in about 1750, when it was taken into cultivation. It reached the United Kingdom in 1763 from Gibraltar. *R. ponticum* is a maid of all work and has had comparatively little influence on the breeding of hybrid rhododendrons with the remarkable exception of 'Hydon Dawn', one of the best of the *R. yakushimanum* hybrids. It is easy to raise from seed and has become naturalized in many parts of Great Britain, where conditions are ideal for its natural re-generation. When it was first grown here, many different forms were selected with different habits of growth and foliage, including variegated forms and many with strangely shaped leaves which earned the description more curious than beautiful. Normally, it is a good foliage plant with dark green leaves, giving an excellent background to other plants, and good for screening and hedging.

The most important role that *R. ponticum* has played in the development of the rhododendron has been as a stock for grafting the hybrids and some of the species. It gives them strong growth, more vigorous than when they are grown on their own roots, and it has been a prime factor in making the hybrids relatively cheap and plentiful. But like any other stock it is liable to throw suckers and it is hard for the average amateur gardener to distinguish these from the cultivated plant. Consequently, they are often left to grow with the result that in time the stock takes over, swamping the scion. In the future this will be less of a problem, as modern methods of propagation, by cuttings and micro-propagation, will mean that more and more rhododendrons will be grown on their own roots.

In spite of the fact that *R. ponticum* has had little general influence on the breeding of rhododendrons, it was one of the parents of the first hybrid, 'Fragrans', which was raised in the Mile End Road Nursery of William Thompson in about 1820. This hybrid used to be known as an *azaleodendron* because its other parent, *R. nudiflorum*, was one of the deciduous azaleas, which were originally classified as a separate genus from rhododendrons. Botanists then realized that there was no clear distinction between the two and that they should all be called rhododendrons; those that lost their leaves forming part of the *azalea* series of the *rhododendron* genus. *R. nudiflorum* came from North America, where it was then known as the 'Pinxterbloom' because it flowered at about Whitsuntide, and Pinxter was the name the colonists gave to that season. It has a strong, attractive scent with rather small flowers of pale pink. 'Fragrans' (not to be confused with 'Fragrantissimum', a scented, tender hybrid for the greenhouse) inherits good points from both parents: it has the scent of *R. nudiflorum* and the evergreen foliage of *R. ponticum*, but with much smaller leaves. It makes a neat, bushy plant, and is also late flowering, thereby missing the spring frosts. Unfortunately, it is not widely grown now and might be difficult to find.

The next species to be introduced to England in 1810 was one of the most important of all. *R. arboreum* came from the Himalayas, where it was discovered by a Captain Hardwicke in 1799, and it is recorded that it first flowered in England at The Grange, Northington, near Alresford in Hampshire, in 1825. The significance of this plant is that it brought the colour red into hybrid rhododendrons and all the early deep-coloured forms derive their colour from this species. Even so, there are many forms of *R. arboreum*, some of them white and spotted and some in various shades of red and pink, but it is not a hardy species and, as with so many plants, the deeper-coloured forms are more tender than the lighter shades. Fortunately, *R. arboreum* has the peculiar characteristic of being able to pass on its rich, deep colours without necessarily handing down its tender constitution at the same time. As the name suggests, it is a very tall-growing rhododendron, sometimes known as the 'Tree Rhododendron of the Himalayas', and this has the effect of making some of the hybrids a little straggly in growth.

Although long since superseded by better cultivars, the basic crosses with the original species flourished for many years and one of these, 'Nobleanum', a hybrid between *R. caucasicum* and *R. arboreum*, was given the Royal Horticultural Society's Award of Garden Merit in 1926. It is a plant that well deserves this prestigious award because it is very early flowering, often with blooms open at Christmas in a mild winter, and it has the fortunate characteristic of being repeat flowering. The buds do not open all at once as with most rhododendrons but come out in succession, and if the early flowers are spoilt by frost, those that are not yet open will come out later. Furthermore, the leaves show the influence of *R. arboreum* and are narrow and pointed, with silvery undersides. The name, 'Nobleanum', suggests that the plant was raised by the firm of Noble and Standish at Sunningdale, but in fact it was bred by Anthony Waterer at Knaphill. When Charles Noble called to see him one day and first saw this plant in flower, he was so full of praise for it, and Anthony Waterer was so flattered, that he gave it his name, latinizing it in the manner of the time.

The other parent of 'Nobleanum', *R. caucasicum*, was the next to be introduced to England. In direct contrast to *R. arboreum* it is a scrub plant from the Caucasus mountains; it came to England as a gift to Sir Joseph Banks from the Russian collector Count Pushkin in 1803. It is somewhat variable in colour; mostly in shades of pink, with some spotted forms, and, curiously, a yellow form, named 'Cunningham's Sulphur', but this is a very poor grower and may not be in cultivation now. *R. caucasicum* is low growing, compact and spreading; it layers itself freely and this quality is passed on to many of its hybrids. As with many of the early species, selected forms were raised and named and one or two of them are still in cultivation: *R. caucasicum* 'Roseum', a good pink form, and *R. caucasicum* 'Pictum' with a definite blotch in the flower. Crossed with *R. ponticum*, *R. caucasicum* produced 'Cunningham's White', which proved to be an excellent plant for tolerating industrial pollution in cities before the Clean Air Act came into force. It can still be seen as large specimens in Birmingham.

R. catawbiense could probably be said to be the species which has made the most important contribution to the success of the rhododendron as a garden plant in the temperate zone because it is known to have withstood 60 degrees of frost where it grows on the banks of the Catawba River in North America. It was discovered by John Fraser and his son when they were collecting plants in North America for the Emperor Paul of Russia, and it first flowered in England in the London nursery of Lee & Kennedy, which is where the Exhibition Hall, Olympia, now stands in Hammersmith. It is a neat, rounded, bushy plant with good foliage, but the flowers are relatively insignificant. They are mauve and both individual floret and truss are rather small, but the plant is late flowering, which gives it immunity from spring frosts. It is still grown today in Europe for sale to the colder parts of North America and northern Europe. Two cultivars that are still obtainable are *R. catawbiense* 'Boursault' (lilac tinged with rose), and *R. catawbiense* 'Grandiflorum' (lilac).

R. campanulatum arrived here from the Himalayas in 1825 but has not been widely used in producing the modern hybrids. The colour varies from pink to purple and some of the purple forms are close to blue. Its neat habit and attractive foliage, dark green above and with a brown underside to the leaf, make it a good plant to grow as an evergreen on its own. The best-known hybrid from it (if it is a hybrid, and not a form of the species) was originally called 'Williams campanulatum hybrid', and is now known as 'Susan'. *R. campanulatum* has probably played a part in the development of the so-called 'blue' hardy hybrids like 'Blue Peter' and 'Blue Ensign', although there is no record of this.

Considering the somewhat mediocre qualities of the early species, it was remarkable that so many good hybrids were produced from them. This was done by careful breeding and selection and, with experience, choosing good parents, which, quite often, did not necessarily have beautiful flowers or good habits of growth themselves. The aims of the early hybridists were summed up by William Watson in his book *Rhododendrons and Azaleas*, published in 1912 in the *Present Day Gardening Series*:

> . . . to raise plants that were hardy, sturdy and shapely in growth, so that when not in flower they were good looking shrubs, whilst the flower heads, to satisfy the requirements of the time, were to be large and full, the flowers holding themselves up, of good substance, the colours pleasing and, most important of all, they were not to expand before June.

The next big break came with the introduction of *R. griffithianum* by Sir Joseph Hooker in 1849. This species is probably one of the most important of them all, ranking with *R. arboreum* and *R. catawbiense*. It has a very lovely flower. Probably the finest description of it was written by Frank Kingdon Ward, who discovered many species in the course of his journeys. In his book *On the Roof of the World* he wrote:

> There is an ethereal quality about the enormous bell flowers – their vital milk-whiteness, their careless rapture of form, their exquisite effortless grace as they hang clustered from the leafy shoots, their subtle fragrance – which defies description.

Even so, *R. griffithianum* is not perfect – it has two faults. First of all, it is not entirely hardy and can only be grown in the open in sheltered gardens in the United Kingdom. It is rather more hardy than *R. arboreum* but has nowhere near the tough constitution of *R. catawbiense*. The other fault is that it is tall growing and inclined to lose the lower leaves. This makes it a leggy plant and occasionally this unfortunate characteristic is passed on to its hybrids.

First crosses with *R. griffithianum* were made with hardy hybrids and one of them, in particular 'Album Elegans', proved to be a good parent, as did one or two more, and the hybridists of the day made full use of these. It has had a considerable influence on modern rhododendrons and the best known of them all is 'Pink Pearl', which owes much of its beauty to *R. griffithianum*. The exact parentage of 'Pink Pearl', still the best known and most popular hybrid rhododendron of them all, is not known for certain. Even the man who introduced it, Gomer Waterer, (it was raised by his father, John Waterer) did not know or, perhaps, would not tell. It is certainly a second generation cross from *R. griffithianum* and has all its good qualities and few of the bad, except the tendency to lose the lower leaves in certain situations. Perhaps one reason for its popularity is its name, which is certainly a good description. 'Pink Pearl' is at its best when it is half open with the deep pink buds standing above the pale pink, fully open flowers. It might well be described as Everyman's rhododendron; it was certainly outstanding when it was introduced at the end of the 19th century, and it was given its first Royal Horticultural Society's Award of Merit in 1897.

It was nearly lost to cultivation because when the first (and only) plant was growing in the trial grounds on the Waterer Nurseries at Bagshot, it was stolen. One day Gomer Waterer was making his regular visit to see the plant as it was coming into flower, and found it had disappeared. This might have seemed like the work of a rival firm, but in fact it had been taken by a workman, who had a fancy to grow it in his front garden. It was later discovered there by Gomer Waterer and brought back to its rightful place.

At about the same time as the Waterers were raising 'Pink Pearl', *R. griffithianum* was being used as a parent by Otto Schultz, Head Gardener at the Royal Porcelain

Factory in Berlin. There it was grown in a greenhouse, where, in truth, it makes a much better plant than it does in the open. He used it with several of the old reds developed from *R. arboreum* to produce a number of hybrids. One of the original crosses is still being grown under the name of 'The Honourable Jean-Marie de Montague'. This is identical to 'Mrs A.M. Williams'; both are bright scarlet with dark green foliage but a rather straggly habit, reflecting the bad side of the character of *R. griffithianum*. In 1896 these hybrids were sold to the Dutch nursery of C.B. van Nes, who made even better use of them, raising such good plants as 'Britannia', 'Unknown Warrior', 'Earl of Athlone', and 'Armistice Day', which were introduced after World War I.

R. fortunei, the first species to come to this country from China, was discovered by Robert Fortune in 1855 when he was on one of his plant-hunting expeditions looking for new varieties of the tea plant to send to India to improve the quality of Indian tea. He happened to spot this beautiful rhododendron on the mountains near Ling Po and made a detour to collect it. When it was discovered to be a species that was entirely new to cultivation, it was given his name. It is more hardy than *R. griffithianum* and the foliage is better, less inclined to fall, and with a very attractive blue sheen. It is a handsome plant out of flower and makes a well-shaped bush. Later, other forms of *R. fortunei* were found. A particularly good one was grown by Sir Edmund Loder at Leonardslee, which he crossed with *R. griffithianum* to produce 'Loderi'. This has even bigger flowers and a bigger truss than either parent. My own opinion is that it is slightly vulgar and the florets that hang down from the truss are more attractive when they can be seen from below on a very large bush. It is also scented, a quality inherited from both parents, but this can be rather heavy and cloying, and not to everyone's taste. Although 'Loderi' is greatly admired by many people, it is not widely grown because until recently almost all rhododendrons were grown by being grafted on *R. ponticum* and my experience would suggest that this is not a suitable stock for any hybrid of *R. fortunei* which is why so few of them are generally available. There are one or two *R. fortunei* hybrids, like 'Lavender Girl', which do not inherit this unfortunate trait of incompatibility with *R. ponticum*, but more could have been grown, had there been a big enough demand, by raising stocks of *R. fortunei* for grafting. However, it is to be hoped that with modern techniques of propagation these rather difficult but often very beautiful hybrids will become more plentiful, less expensive and more widely grown.

Another species collected in the Himalayas by Sir Joseph Hooker on his successful expedition of 1849 was *R. thomsonii*. This has also had some influence on the development of the popular hybrids, and is an attractive species in its own right. It is tall-growing with rounded leaves and very attractive, orange-brown bark, which is no small part of the plant's beauty. The blood-red flowers are cup shaped and have large calyces. Many of the *R. thomsonii* seeds brought back to England by Sir Joseph Hooker were raised in the Berkshire nurseries of Standish and Noble, who were so intrigued by this plant that they found a way of making it flower much sooner than if it had been left to its own devices. By grafting some scions onto a very old standard rhododendron they were able to produce flowers within a few years, and used these to raise 'Ascot Brilliant', which was introduced in 1861, only 12 years after the species was first recorded. 'Ascot Brilliant', the best-known hybrid of *R. thomsonii* and still widely grown, has the same colour as its parent and similarities in foliage and shape of flower. *R. thomsonii* flowers early, usually in March or April, but 'Ascot Brilliant', due to the influence of its other, unknown parent, is much later, usually opening at the end of April or in early May.

In a way, the introduction of *R. thomsonii* could be said to mark the end of an era, the period of exploration in the Himalayas, which had brought many fine new species into cultivation. These plants had improved the quality of the hybrids produced from the original North American and European species and from the first Himalayan rhododendron of them all, *R. arboreum*.

The next major introduction came in 1917 and was *R. griersonianum*, which was discovered by George Forrest at a height of 3,000 metres in western Yunnan, China. This rhododendron was at first thought to be even more important than previous discoveries because of its very pure scarlet colour. The red forms of *R. arboreum* have a faint underlying tone of blue and, together with the blue that comes from *R. catawbiense*, this tends to result in a somewhat coarse shade of red, lacking the clear scarlet found, for example, in many of the zonal pelargoniums. Consequently, *R. griersonianum* was enthusiastically welcomed by the amateur raisers of new rhododendron hybrids in the years immediately following World War I. But to paraphrase Matthew Prior they were 'to its virtues ever kind and to its faults a little blind'. In spite of growing at a high altitude in the wild, it turned out to be somewhat tender, largely because it grew late into the summer, and even into autumn, and the young growth tended to be cut by early frosts. Its growth in cultivation was very loose and unkempt, probably because, like *R. hirsutum*, it prefers the more rigorous conditions of its natural habitat. Although many crosses were made with *R. griersonianum*, most exist only as single specimens in private collections and very few have survived as popular garden plants. Not surprisingly, the only one that became generally popular was 'Earl of Donoughmore', raised and introduced by a Dutchman, Peter Koster, in 1953. This undoubtedly carries the colour of *R. griersonianum* but, unfortunately, proved to be almost as tender as the other crosses.

Finally, we come to *R. yakushimanum*, the finest of all the rhododendron species that have played a part in the development of the modern hybrid. This species is unrivalled by any previous discovery, and it is, I believe, so outstanding that nothing better will ever be found. Furthermore, I doubt there will ever be a hybrid raised from it to equal the true plant. Any attempt to improve on its perfection would result in something being lost, probably the most important characteristic of all, the beautiful proportions of the plant in all aspects – shape, leaf, young growth, and the very delicate form of the flowers.

R. yakushimanum was first described by the Japanese botanist T. Naki in 1920 and two plants were sent to Lionel de Rothschild at Exbury by the Japanese botanist and nurseryman Dr Koichiro Wada in 1932. It was first seen by the public when it was exhibited by the Commissioners of Crown Lands at the Chelsea Flower Show of 1948. It caused considerable interest, particularly among rhododendron enthusiasts, and at one time there were more articles being written about it than there were plants in the United Kingdom. The great question was – is it a true species, a form of a species, or perhaps a natural hybrid? These doubts were raised because the plant does not come true from seed, as a pure species would, and there was a difference between the two plants that had been sent to Lionel de Rothschild. One of them, which is now in the Gardens of the Royal Horticultural Society at Wisley, has more rounded leaves than the other but is slightly paler in the colour of the flower. In the end it was considered that the best of the two was the form at Wisley, which received a First Class Certificate. This form was then given the clonal name of *R. yakushimanum* FCC 'Koichiro Wada'. It would be hard to think of a more difficult and cumbersome name, but it is right that Dr Wada should be so honoured for he has made a prodigious contribution to decorative gardening.

The rhododendrons described in this chapter are the principal species that have played a part in the development of the hardy hybrids, the type that is the popular conception of the rhododendron. But there are many more: from *R. camtschaticum* , a tiny, creeping plant only a few inches high, which grows as far north as Alaska and the Aleutians, to *R. sinogrande*, which grows in China, Burma and Tibet and has been known to have leaves 2ft 6in (0.75m) long and 1ft (0.3m) or more wide. Both of these beautiful and interesting species require special conditions to succeed, but they are mentioned here as illustrations of the variety of rhododendrons that can be grown in the British Isles.

CULTIVATION

Rhododendrons are easy to grow, but despite this they do not always flourish as garden plants, unless, of course, the owner is an enthusiast. They are sometimes seen at their best in the most unlikely situations, but fail in others where conditions would seem to be far better. Among the many possible reasons for this, one might be that rhododendrons have a justifiable reputation for being tough plants that need little attention, and consequently get less attention than they deserve.

Situation

The amount of sun or shade sometimes affects their welfare and for the majority of hardy hybrids the ideal is that they should have their tops in sun and their roots in shade. The best way to provide this is by planting them in a group or groups so that they offer each other mutual shade, as they do when growing in the wild. This is sometimes decried by garden designers and landscape gardeners, who object to what they call 'monocultures of rhododendrons', but it is often the occasional, single plant in private gardens that seems to suffer more than most. Some cultivars, mostly the bright reds and scarlets, need shade because the flowers are inclined to fade in sunlight and, if possible, it is better to place these where they are shaded from the heat of the midday sun. Those that flower early in the year, any time before mid-May, are better in a position where they are shaded from early morning sun. There are few districts where rhododendrons can be grown that are immune from spring frosts, and flowers can be damaged if they receive direct sunlight while they are still frosted.

Soil

Rhododendrons must have an acid soil, and if they are being planted for the first time, the local flora is often a good guide to the type of soil. Heather, gorse, pine trees, and silver birch all indicate an acid soil, in which it will be safe to plant rhododendrons without having to change it either physically or chemically. The scientific method is to test the soil with one of the simple, relatively inexpensive soil-test kits that are now available. These indicate the degree of acidity, measured in terms of the symbol pH, by comparing the colour of a solution when soil has been added to it with a chart provided. It is worth while using one of these kits because it has been found, comparatively recently, that soil can be too acid for rhododendrons, resulting in the same effect – chlorotic foliage and stunted growth – as when they are planted in alkaline soils. Where the soil is very acid, it is sometimes even necessary to add lime. A pH reading of 5.6 is now generally regarded as being the optimum reading for rhododendrons.

It is possible to change the acidity of the soil in various ways. If it is close to neutral, without any definite lime content, the addition of plenty of peat or leaf mould and well-rotted cow manure, with frequent mulches of the same, will be enough to make it possible to grow rhododendrons. Soil can also be made more acid by the use of Copperas (ferrous sulphate), applied to the surface at the rate of 5lb (2.26kg) per 100sq ft (9.3sq m) and well watered in. This will need to be monitored, and further applications made if necessary. Tests should be carried out twice a year.

On soils which are either neutral or only slightly alkaline it is possible to achieve limited success with the use of an iron-chelating agent. Rhododendrons will not grow on a lime soil because the iron is locked out causing them to become chlorotic and make very poor growth. The chelating agent 'grabs' the iron in the soil and makes it available to the plant. Unfortunately, this is a somewhat expensive procedure as the chemicals are costly and regular applications are necessary.

For an alkaline soil probably a more satisfactory method is to provide raised beds; these are above the normal level of the soil and contain prepared acid soil for the plants. Replacing alkaline with acid soil in an ordinary bed is not advisable because eventually the lime will seep through from the surrounding ground and reduce the acidity of the imported soil. Raised beds can be an attractive feature, particularly if they are made with peat blocks, and small ericaceous plants are set in the interstices to bind the blocks together.

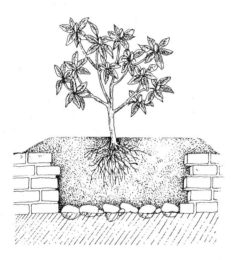

The most satisfactory way of growing rhododendrons on a lime soil is to make up a bed of suitable acid soil above the surface of the lime soil. This prevents the risk of lime seeping through and creating alkaline conditions.

Planting

Preparation of the soil Acid soils are often thin and hungry, and because rhododendrons grow in an acid soil it is often thought that they will thrive in a poor soil. This is not so. The best soil for rhododendrons is an acid loam with plenty of body, similar to the rich seam that runs along the Weald of Kent, where some of the finest rhododendron gardens in England can be found. Rhododendrons like plenty of moisture but they do not like to be in waterlogged soil. Again, there are ideal conditions along the Weald of Kent, where in many places small springs on the high ground provide moisture which drains away to the valleys below.

These perfect conditions are not found everywhere. This means that the soil must be well prepared to provide food and moisture. This should be done some time before planting takes place. Even though rhododendrons are surface rooting, the ground should be dug at least two spits deep, and over a wide area, allowing at least a 4ft (1.2m) square for each plant. This will ensure good drainage and will give the soil time to settle. It should also be enriched with peat; natural bracken peat, although this is now in short supply, is preferable to sphagnum moss peat. The plants also need feeding and the best basic feed to incorporate with the soil is well-rotted cow manure. Nowadays it can be dangerous to obtain cow manure from dairy farms where powerful disinfectants are used to wash out cow sheds and milking parlours. These take a long time to biodegrade and it is better, if possible, to obtain cow manure from stockyards and calf pens where hygiene does not demand the frequent use of disinfectants. It is important also to use only cow manure as that of pigs or horses contains too much free ammonia which can cause leaf scorch.

Spacing It is difficult to give a general rule about spacing rhododendrons in a border because so much depends on the habit and rate of growth of individual cultivars. Even so, a good general rule is that plants should never be closer than 5ft (1.5m) apart each way in their permanent positions. Their close fibrous roots make them easy to transplant, so another way is to plant a little closer, about 4ft (1.2m) apart, and later transplant some, leaving the rest in their permanent positions. If only small plants are available, the borders will look rather thin at first. This can be overcome by planting among the rhododendrons other flowering shrubs, which can be removed or transplanted later.

Planting Because they are surface rooting many rhododendrons fail through being planted too deeply. The bottom of the hole should be well forked over and firmed, and the plant should be placed so that the top of the root ball is level with the top of the hole and no deeper. Some peat or well-rotted leaf-mould should be put round the roots before starting to backfill, which should then be done in stages, and the earth well trodden in and firmed. If the ground is wet or heavy, the plants should be set higher than the level of the soil, and the soil and peat built up around them, making sure that the whole planting area is covered with soil and peat to the same height, and not built up in little heaps around individual plants.

Planting can take place at any time from September to March, but the best results will be from autumn planting. However, it is possible to plant rhododendrons right up to the time when they start their growth – and even later if they have been grown in containers and are kept well watered after planting.

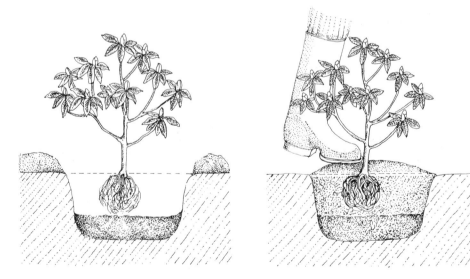

It is important not to plant too deeply. The rhododendron should be set at the same depth that it was growing before, and the cultivated soil below should be firmed to prevent sinking.

Firm planting is one of the secrets of success.

Aftercare

Feeding At one time the rule used to be that no artificial fertilizers should be given to rhododendrons in any form, but nowadays experience has shown that, with care, some can be used. Even so, it is probably safer to keep to organic feeding, which has always been effective in the past, until current experimental work has been well tried in practice.

Organic feeding is done by mulching, and the best mulch of all is a specially prepared heap, made up with layers of peat or leaf-mould and well-rotted cow manure, and left to stand, preferably for two years. This mulch then cuts like cheese and can be broken up and placed round the plants at a distance from the stem equivalent to their height. This may be done in the winter or early spring, and the soil should be moist at the time, otherwise the mulch might prevent the rain from penetrating to the roots.

If it is not possible to provide that ideal diet of rotted manure and peat or leaf-mould, there are several other mulches that can be used. Surprisingly, I have found from my own experience that it is possible to mulch rhododendrons with fresh grass cuttings to good effect. At one time this was thought to be dangerous but I have found that this is not so. Needless to say, they can only be used for this purpose provided that no selective weedkillers have been applied to the grass. Garden compost will also make a suitable mulch, but only if neither lime nor an activator containing lime has been used in the heap. Bracken and straw can also be effective in conserving moisture and providing shade for the young roots. Spent hops, available from some garden centres, make a good mulch; their only shortcoming is that they contain little plant food, even less than that contained in rotted farmyard manure.

When it comes to direct feeding, dried chicken manure, well rotted down and preferably with the addition of superphosphate, will give both phosphorus and nitrogen in a natural form, but it must be emphasized that it should be well rotted and dry. There are a number of proprietary manures made up from rotted chicken manure, which are also suitable.

An occasional problem with rhododendrons is lack of flower bud. This can be overcome by giving a high nitrogen feed in March, using sulphate of ammonia sprinkled on at the rate of 2oz (57gm) to 1sq yd (0.8sq m). This will encourage good strong growth at the start, which helps the plants to grow away well and develop flower bud. The extra vigour given by a nitrogen feed can also help to combat the effects of late spring frosts,

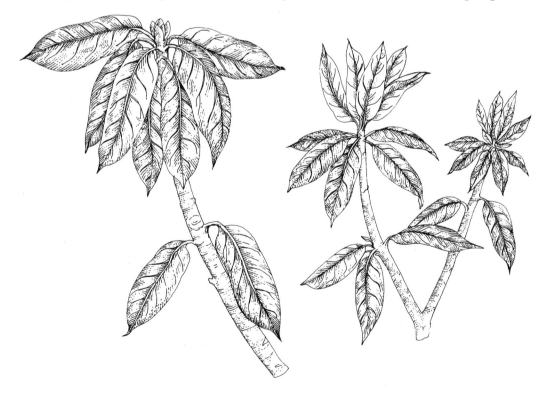

A warm, wet summer will cause rhododendrons to make secondary growth, growing out through the flower bud. This will cause leggy growth, which will need to be pruned in the following spring.

which all too often can cut the first growth. However, on no account should nitrogen in any form be given to rhododendrons after the end of May, as it might encourage them to make late, soft growth, which would be vulnerable to early autumn frosts. The use of superphosphate, at the same rate as for sulphate of ammonia, has also been found to encourage flower buds to set. Potash feeds have been used in America but they need considerable care and accurate measuring, which makes them somewhat dangerous. Too much can cause severe damage to the plant, even death.

Weeding Fortunately for rhododendrons the annual ritual of digging over shrub borders to make them clean and tidy for the winter has been abandoned in favour of mulching generally to keep down the weeds. Sawdust has been used for this but it is not to be recommended as it is inclined to encourage fungus diseases and it 'robs as it rots', that is, it takes up nitrogen from the soil in the process of rotting down. The modern chipped bark mulches are preferable because they do not rot down quickly and they provide good cover to keep the weeds down and conserve moisture.

There should be no cultivation at all among the roots of rhododendrons because, as they are surface rooting, a great deal of damage will be done even by shallow hoeing. To a certain extent rhododendrons provide their own mulch from their own fallen leaves and it is curious that other fallen leaves seem also naturally to collect under rhododendrons.

The acid nature of rhododendrons inhibits weed growth underneath the plants, and if they are arranged carefully, with low-growing, bushy, spreading plants round the outside of the group, there is no need to use ground-cover plants. These can have a bad effect on rhododendrons by taking away valuable food and moisture from the top of the soil where they most need it. A weed that is a natural and beneficial companion to rhododendrons is *Claytonia perfoliata*, known as American chickweed, and this is now being grown as a salad crop. Its advantage to rhododendrons is that it has a very small root system and a large top growth, which covers the ground and keeps it moist. If it appears naturally in the garden, it is an indication that the soil is exactly right for rhododendrons, and because of its shallow root system, it is easy to control.

Deadheading The most essential operation in growing rhododendrons is to deadhead the flowers as soon as they have faded. Failure to do this is probably the most widespread cause of unhealthy plants. The effect of bearing a heavy crop of seed is not only debilitating but also a prime cause of lack of flower bud in the following year. It is important that the flowers should be picked off as early as possible in order to avoid damage to the embryo growth buds, which are just below the flower head and will provide the flower buds for the following year. The dead truss should be picked off cleanly at the point where it joins the stem. Most of them come away easily but some are more difficult and need careful handling. A good tip is to stand on the north side of the bush because the flowers always tend to grow towards the sun; they can then be bent backwards, which gives a clean break at the joint. Any dead or damaged buds still on the bushes should also be picked off, as they may be a contributory factor to the disease of bud blast.

Suckering Until recently suckering (removing the growth which may come up from the *R. ponticum* root stock) has been as important as deadheading. If the strong growth of *R. ponticum* is left to compete with the cultivated plant which has been grafted on to it, it will eventually take over and swamp the whole bush. Modern methods of propagation, by cuttings or by micro-propagation, will eventually eliminate this difficulty completely, but until all rhododendrons are grown of their own roots, it is still necessary to watch out for suckers on grafted plants.

This means it is necessary to know how the plants you buy have been propagated. If they are known to be on their own roots, there is no problem, but if they are likely to have been grafted, a careful watch must be kept on the growth coming up from below.

Unfortunately, it is difficult to distinguish between the young growth of *R. ponticum* and that of a cultivated hybrid. As the growth matures, *R. ponticum* can be recognized by its narrow, dark green leaves and vigorous growth, but then, regrettably, it is almost too late to remove the sucker without damage.

If the plant is definitely known to have been grafted, then all growth coming from below the ground should be removed. By chopping downwards with a sharp spade or a suckering tool, the sucker should be broken off cleanly at the root. It is important not to cut the sucker with a knife because this will only make it more vigorous and, later, more difficult to remove.

Pruning Unlike roses or fruit trees, rhododendrons do not need regular pruning. It only needs to be done when they grow straggly or become badly overcrowded. There are certain hybrids which grow so strongly that they may need to be cut back every seven to ten years, depending on their condition. Some of these are 'Corry Koster', 'General Eisenhower', 'George Hardy', 'John Waterer', 'Louis Pasteur', 'Marchioness of Lansdowne', 'Moser's Maroon', 'Princess Elizabeth', 'Professor Zayer'.

Regrettably, the best time to prune is in March or April, which means the loss of at least one year's flower. When rhododendrons need pruning, they must be pruned completely, leaving no foliage. They should be cut right back into good healthy wood, on average $\frac{1}{2}$in (13mm) in diameter. If they are only partially pruned, the whole effort of the plant will go into the branches that are left, and the result will be worse than it was before. Accordingly, plants should be cut back to make a regular shape, which will become a sound basis for future growth. The rhododendrons that need pruning will be the strong growers which often make a second or even a third growth in a season, and they should be cut at the point where this second growth has started. On the stem there is a definite ring surrounded by very small nascent growth buds, which appear as little pimples. The cuts should be made just above this point so that the plant breaks into growth without leaving a stump of dead wood where there might be no dormant growth buds.

Rhododendrons should never be pruned unless they are in good health and growing strongly. They need to be established for at least three years and if they are not in really good condition, they should be fed beforehand with sulphate of ammonia to ensure that their subsequent growth will be strong and that they will be able to break out from the tiny growth buds just showing through the bark. Once the pruned plants break out and make their first year's growth, some parts will grow so strongly that in order to create a well-balanced plant it may be necessary to pinch out some growth buds to check particular branches.

Most rhododendrons may be pruned with safety, but there are some that do not break from the old wood easily and it is wise to leave these alone. A list from my own experience is as follows: 'Alice', 'Bagshot Ruby', 'C.B. van Nes', 'Concessum Master', 'Concessum', 'Grand Arab', 'J.H. Agnew', 'Mrs C.B. van Nes', 'Prometheus' and 'Nobleanum' cultivars.

Container cultivation

Rhododendrons grow surprisingly well in containers, which can be used to good effect in a number of ways. They can provide a solution to the problem of an alkaline soil. The container can be plunged in the ground, giving the rhododendron the appearance of a normal growing plant, but the container will protect the roots from any damaging infusion of lime. Rhododendrons in containers can also be brought into the house, where they can make an effective and even dramatic display, either forced into flower early or allowed to flower normally. Almost any container will do, but it is wise to avoid those made of cement or concrete, particularly if they are porous. Lime is again the reason, for if the roots were to penetrate the material, the plants might suffer. Because rhododendrons are surface rooting it is better to choose containers that are short and fat rather than tall and thin; this allows room both for the roots to spread and for the application of a mulch to feed them.

When plants have been pruned they sometimes make extra growth after the first flush. This should be trimmed back, as shown, or the original pruning will become ineffective, resulting in leggy growth.

When pruning cut just above a normal growth bud yet not so far above it as to leave a stub of wood, nor so close as to damage the bud. The cut should be as short as possible, at right angles to the growth, and not slanting.

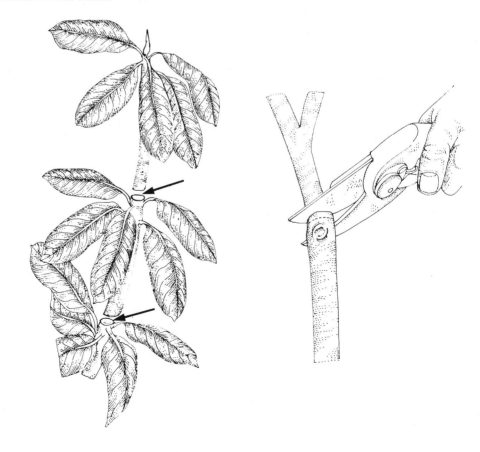

25

Good drainage is important. Container-grown plants from garden centres should be re-potted, placing concave crocks over the holes in the pot and then a layer of coarse peat or leaf-mould. Any of the composts for ericaceous plants will be suitable, although one made from coarser materials will give better results. A good mixture is three parts peat or leaf-mould, two parts limefree loam, one part well-rotted cow manure, and roughly a handful of Perlite to every two gallons (9.09l) of the mixture. This mixture should be carefully broken down by hand into a convenient grade for potting. It should not be sieved because then it will settle down too tightly and become compacted. Enough space for watering should be left at the top of the container.

Watering is the most important part of growing rhododendrons in containers. There is always a risk that very hard water will add sufficient lime to the compost to cause damage to the plant. This will depend on the relative acidity of the local water supply and if it is above neutral (pH 7), it is advisable to use only rain water, or that from a pond or stream, provided that it is pH 7 or below. This warning is only likely to be necessary in an extreme situation where the water is definitely alkaline. Otherwise the very acid nature of the compost will last for many years, usually until the plant needs to be transferred to a larger container. During the flowering and growing period rhododendrons need plenty of water but should not become water-logged. Once they have made their growth, they need only enough water to keep them in good condition, but they should never be allowed to dry out. The reason for this is that once they have grown and started to make flower bud for the following year, they need to harden off to retain that flower bud. If they are then encouraged to make further growth by too much water, they will grow through that flower bud, and the new, soft growth would be both vulnerable to an early autumn frost and unlikely to set a second crop of buds.

Rhododendrons may be forced into flower easily and even the protection of a cold greenhouse will bring them on a good fortnight ahead of their normal time. They should not be brought in under glass until they have suffered a slight frost in the open. They will then react more readily to the kinder conditions, and a little heat and regular sprays with warm water will make them flower even earlier. They should not be shaded when they are first brought in under glass, but it is important to do this at the beginning of April when the sun can be strong enough to burn the leaves in a greenhouse.

Many cultivars adapt well to container cultivation, and a selection of plants that have a compact habit, early flowers, or attractive foliage is given in the Recommended Varieties lists.

DISEASES, PESTS AND DISORDERS

Many of the pests of rhododendrons and, to a very limited extent, some of the fungal diseases can be controlled by spraying. When dealing with pests it is important to spray underneath the leaves almost more than on top, because that is where most of the insects live and lay their eggs. Complete coverage is required and the most satisfactory way of obtaining this is by ultra-low volume spraying with the use of a suitable atomizing sprayer, one of the most effective being the Turbair Series now distributed and maintained by Pan Britannica Industries.

When using chemical pesticides, always take extreme care. Always follow manufacturer's instructions carefully for quantities, dilutions and so on. Similarly always wash your hands (or preferably use gloves), and wash the equipment. Do not store any leftover solutions, and do not transfer the chemical into other storage containers, especially beer and soft drink bottles.

Diseases

Bud blast This fungal disease (*Pycnostysanus (Sporocybe) azaleae*) is the most difficult of all to combat. One of the reasons for this is that in the initial stages it is very similar to winter frost damage on flower buds. Buds first become slightly discoloured, then gradually turn black, and in the final stages are covered in short hairs. However, the buds remain on the bushes, which is not only unsightly but can have the added danger of spreading the disease.

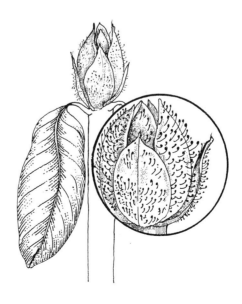

The hairs on the buds distinguish the disease bud blast from frost damage. The only remedy is to pick off affected buds and burn them.

There is a theory that the leaf hopper is largely responsible for bud blast. This may or may not be true, but at present the only control for bud blast is to pick off the dead buds and burn them. This is a somewhat difficult operation where there are large plantations, but there is really no satisfactory alternative.

Powdery mildew This is the latest fungal disease to attack rhododendrons. It was first discovered in the United States and has only recently come to the British Isles in, so far, limited areas. Very little is known about it and no cure has been found. The leaves first become covered with the powdery mildew, and then shrivel up and fall off. So far, the best course of action seems to be picking off the leaves and burning them. Fungicides can be applied, particularly Benlate and Maneb, but they have the disadvantage of leaving a heavy white deposit on all the leaves, whether affected or not, which is rather disfiguring. Fungicides primarily intended for the control of powdery mildews on cereal crops have also been found to be effective on rhododendrons and azaleas. These are imazalil and dimethylformamide.

Honey fungus This fungus (*Armillaria mellea),* known also as bootlace fungus and shoe-string fungus, can attack many trees and shrubs, and rhododendrons are particularly susceptible when grown in woodland, where fallen branches, leaf-mould and rotting wood can be contributory factors. The first sign will be a general deterioration in the health of the plant. On closer examination it will be seen that fungus in the form of small black tentacles is fanning out on the bark of the plant at soil level. These then develop into strands, rather like bootlaces, which give the disease one of its common names. To clear it you can change or sterilize the soil before replanting. There are two preparations that will check the honey fungus: Bray's Emulsion and Armillotox, which should be used according to the manufacturer's instructions.

Pests

Leaf hopper This insect (*Graphocephala coccinea* Forster) was identified by G. Fox Wilson, then entomologist to the Royal Horticultural Society, who gave the opinion that although it appeared to pierce the buds and even to feed on them, it caused no visible damage. But in a note in the 1937 *Yearbook of the Rhododendron Association* he added:

> The invasion of secondary agents (fungoid and bacterial organisms) through the feeding punctures of the insects may prove to be more serious than the feeding of the insect itself.

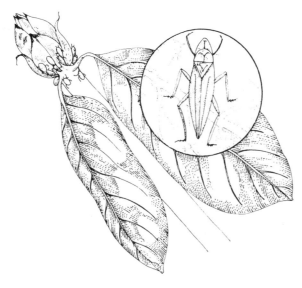

Although the leaf hopper pierces the buds, this does not have any immediate effect. It is thought that the punctures may be a contributory factor in the incidence of bud blast, which makes it advisable to kill the leaf hopper by spraying.

The first sign of the presence of the vine weevil may well be the damage to the leaves. Trap or destroy as described.

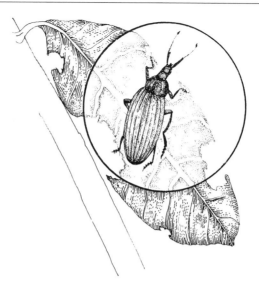

This, needless to say, gives strength to the idea that the leaf hopper does have some effect on the spread of bud blast.

The leaf hopper can be controlled by spraying with any insecticide containing permethrin, backed up by a later spray containing dimethoate, a systemic insecticide.

Greenfly This common pest (*Aphis*) can attack plants by feeding on the young growth, which, when it develops, becomes first distorted, as though damaged by frost, and then stunted with small leaves. This is particularly disfiguring because not all branches are attacked, which makes those affected look worse than they otherwise might.

As with all aphid attacks early action goes a long way towards eradicating the pest. It is wise to carry an aerosol spray of any good aphid killer in the pocket during the time the nymphs are hatching, usually late April, and to deal with any outbreak as soon as it is seen. This can be very effective where there are relatively few plants but in large plantations it will be necessary to spray with an insecticide containing permethrin followed by dimethoate.

Lacewing fly This pest (*Leptobyres (Stephanites) rhododendri* Horv) is also known as the rhododendron fly. The first sign of its presence will probably be a pattern of small yellow dots on the leaves. These are caused by the punctures made by the adults when they lay their eggs in the leaves. Unfortunately, by then it is too late to do anything about it for that particular season. When the eggs hatch out in the following year, usually in June, the lacewing fly starts as the rhododendron bug, a small crawling insect on the underside of the leaves which become sticky with the hatching eggs. It is better to stop them even before they have hatched out, because as they develop they grow wings and move up into the young growth to lay their eggs. If they can be kept out of the young growth for a couple of years, it is possible to eradicate them entirely.

If the lacewing fly is allowed to remain on plants unchecked, it can cause poor growth and, in extreme cases, death. A vigilant watch should be kept for those tell-tale yellow spots and any affected leaves should be picked off and burnt. If the attack becomes more serious, permethrin followed by dimethoate is once more the best remedy. If a plant is very seriously affected, it may be necessary to prune it right back, cutting out and burning the infested leaves and branches.

Vine weevil This pest (*Otiorhynchus sulcatus*) has become more prevalent in recent years, not only on rhododendrons but also on other evergreen shrubs. The early flowering cultivars are more vulnerable than other rhododendrons, probably because the insects appear in April and early May when the early flowering cultivars are making their first growth. The fully grown vine weevil is about ½in (13mm) long, black, and with elbowed whiskers on its short snout. It appears to have wings, but it cannot fly. It is not easy to see, largely because it feeds on the plants during the night and hides on the ground among stones, dead leaves and debris during the day. Mulching, although necessary for feeding the plants, inevitably provides the pest with a good resting place during the daytime. The first signs of an attack by the vine weevil are usually circular and evenly spaced cuts in the leaves. The insect lays its eggs in the soil near the base of the plant and they later develop into larvae, which feed from the soil and roots.

The one certain chemical cure, which will kill adults, eggs and larvae, is the soil pesticide Aldrin but it is only available at present to commercial growers. The alternatives are to use Murphy's Tumblebug for the adult insect and their Rootguard or Fison's Soil Pest Killer for the larvae and eggs, following the instructions on the packets.

The fully grown insects may be trapped by placing pieces of sacking and crumpled paper at the base of the plants during the evening, then collecting them and burning them in the daytime, when the insects will have gone to rest in the traps. A biological control has been found by a Dutch nurseryman, who runs a flock of bantams among his plants and they seek out and eat both adults and larvae. Sadly, this is not practicable in the average private garden.

Rhododendron whitefly This pest (*Daileurodes chittendeni* Laing) is not serious and causes little damage to rhododendrons except that the small white-winged insects, which look rather weak and feeble, exude a form of honeydew that settles on the leaves and provides a base for the growth of sooty moulds, thereby making the plants somewhat unsightly. It can be more prevalent under protection than in the open, but control is not difficult by spraying with an insecticide containing permethrin.

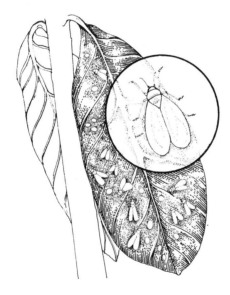

Whitefly can cause deposits of sooty moulds on the foliage. Spray as directed.

Disorders
Bark split This problem, which affects other ornamental shrubs and fruit trees as well as rhododendrons, occurs when the bark splits open, at best leaving a scar, at worst causing the death of young plants. It is a little difficult to isolate the conditions that cause it , but it happens most often as the result of an early autumn frost, while the sap is still high in the plant, or a late spring frost, when the sap has already started to rise. When the bark is frozen, the rising sap cannot get through, and then the bark splits to a greater or lesser

Bark splitting proves fatal only on very young plants. It disfigures older specimens, but the effect can be made less severe by dressing with grafting wax or one of the preparations sold for treating pruning wounds.

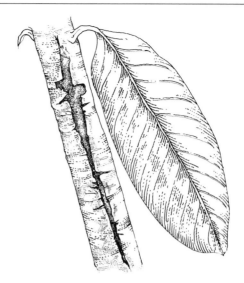

degree. For this reason it is dangerous to give a nitrogenous feed to rhododendrons after the end of May because it could have the effect of stimulating growth through to the autumn, when there is always a risk of an early frost.

Some cultivars are more prone to bark split than others, and where this is known, a low rating for the hardiness of the wood has been given in the descriptions of the plants concerned. As a general rule, those with a high proportion of the sap of *R. griffithianum*, and some of those with a similar inheritance from *R. arboreum*, are at more risk than others. But this is by no means a hard and fast rule; the breeding of modern rhododendrons is so complicated that a particular cultivar may appear to have a high proportion of the qualities of *R. griffithianum* and yet have inherited hardiness from a stronger species way back in its ancestry.

Regrettably, there is little that can be done to prevent bark split although the wounds may be helped to heal over by the application of grafting wax or any of the preparations that are available to ameliorate the effects of hard pruning.

Failure to set flower bud It is particularly disappointing to have rhododendrons which appear to be growing well yet fail to give a good show of flower. Quite often the very health and vigour of the plant is the cause of lack of flower bud. The solution is to prune the roots by cutting round them with a spade, or to lift the plant and re-plant it. This will give a check to the strong growth and will encourage the production of flower bud.

Others factors may also inhibit the production of flower bud. Failure to deadhead as soon as the flowers are over can cause poor flowering in the following year. Or the plant may be in a position with too much shade, which would prevent the sunlight from hardening the wood. Or cold, wet weather during June and July can cause the flower buds to grow through, that is, turn into new growth that may not mature sufficiently to induce a second flower bud.

31

HARDINESS RATINGS

These are given for the different parts of the plant as indicated below. The star rating refers only to hardiness of one sort or another and is no indication of the intrinsic merits of the plant. It does give some idea of the situation that is most suitable for a particular plant.

For example, 'A. Bedford' has a low rating for its foliage because the leaves are subject to damage by wind and sun – avoid draughts and full exposure from midday onward. The same applies to 'Beauty of Littleworth'.

'Fragrantissimum' has a low rating on all counts and can be grown only in the open in very mild areas, otherwise it must be treated as a greenhouse plant.

Bud Some rhododendrons may be quite hardy in flower but make their growth so late in the year that sometimes the bud does not harden off enough to withstand an early autumn frost.

Flower This rating is for the hardiness of the flower when it is fully developed and free of the bud scales. Obviously the later flowering cultivars receive a high grading under this column because they are not subjected to such severe frosts as the more early flowering sorts. The early flowering cultivars are judged in comparison with one another.

Wood One of the trials of rhododendron growers is a disorder known as 'bark split'. This is the result of frost affecting the plant when the sap is rising. Some cultivars are more prone to this than others, particularly those with a strong strain of *R. griffithianum*.

Foliage The foliage rating is based on the ability of the leaves to stand hot sunshine as well as frost. It is hard to differentiate between the two and, many varieties, those that do not stand frost well, are apt also to be burned by the sun. Part shade helps.

Flowering period Different species and cultivars may be found in flower from Christmas until August, but most of them flower from the third week in April to the end of June. It is difficult to predict the time of flowering within this period for individual plants, as so much depends on the season, and even the same plant will vary from year to year. A rough indication is given for each plant illustrated as follows:

Early – end of April to the beginning of May

Mid-season – May

Late – end of May to early June

Any exceptions to these periods have been noted in the captions.

Size It is difficult to indicate the ultimate size of the different species and cultivars as so much depends on the situation in which they are grown. The majority of the plants illustrated will grow to around 4–5ft (1.2–1.5m) under average garden conditions in 8 to 10 years from a young plant 12–15in (30–38cm) high. Exceptions are noted in the text, for example 'A. Bedford' – 'tall growing' because of its faster rate of growth. Those described as 'dwarf' and 'suitable for the rock garden' are small in all their parts – habit, leaf, flower and truss.

Rhododendron flowers, perhaps more than those of any other plant, vary greatly in colour depending on the time of year and in which part of the country they are grown. The illustrations on the pages that follow reflect that variety and so may not necessarily have quite the same colour as a plant you know or have grown.

RHS's GARDENS AT WISLEY
A general view of
rhododendron trials at the
Royal Horticultural Society's
gardens at Wisley. This world
famous garden is one of the
finest places to see some of the
new introductions which
have been selected for trial
and many of the old
established hybrids and
species.

WILGENS RUBY

'Wilgens Ruby', also known as 'Van Wilgens Ruby', was raised by A. C. van Wilgens in Boskoop and received a First Class Certificate in the trials there in 1951. It might well be described as a modern hardy hybrid cast in the old mould. The reason for this is that it is very hardy, has a good, bushy, compact habit with dark green foliage, and it sets flower bud freely. It is one of the best rhododendrons to have been produced in Boskoop since the end of World War II.

Bud ✱✱✱✱ Flower ✱✱✱✱
Wood ✱✱✱✱ Foliage ✱✱✱✱
Flowering: late

PERCY WISEMAN

'Percy Wiseman' is one of the more successful hybrids from *R. yakushimanum* and was raised by Percy Wiseman himself, for many years manager of the Waterer nursery at Bagshot. It is a very attractive plant of good, bushy habit, but with only just a suggestion of yellow in its flower. Percy Wiseman was a man of considerable knowledge having trained originally in France. When he took over as manager of the Bagshot nursery it became one of the most efficient production nurseries in the country.

Bud ✱✱✱✱ Flower ✱✱✱
Wood ✱✱✱✱ Foliage ✱✱✱✱
Flowering: mid-season

PROFESSOR HUGO DE VRIES
'Professor Hugo de Vries' was
raised by the Dutch nursery of
L. J. Endtz, and is the result of
a cross between 'Doncaster'
and 'Pink Pearl'. This was
another, largely successful
attempt to improve upon
'Pink Pearl' by giving it a
deeper colour yet retaining
the same size of flower and
truss. A similar attempt was
made by R. White of the
Sunningdale nurseries by
crossing 'Pink Pearl' with
'Cynthia' to raise 'Countess of
Derby'. Strangely enough,
'Countess of Derby' and
'Professor Hugo de Vries' are
almost identical,
distinguishable only by the
eye of an expert. If anything,
'Countess of Derby' has a
rather better habit than
'Professor Hugo de Vries',
which is somewhat surprising
seeing that 'Doncaster' is a
more bushy grower than
'Cynthia'.

Bud ★★★ Flower ★★★★
Wood ★★★★ Foliage ★★★★
Flowering: mid-season

FORTUNE

'Fortune' was one of Lionel de Rothschild's greatest achievements. It is a cross between *R. falconeri* and *R. sinogrande*, which received a First Class Certificate in 1938. It is a very striking plant, growing nearly as tall as its parents to 20–30ft (6.1–9.1m), with leaves 16in (41cm) long and wide in proportion. The yellow flowers are often carried 25 to a truss which makes it altogether a very impressive plant.

Bud   **   Flower **
Wood **   Foliage **
Flowering: early

GOLDSWORTH CRIMSON
'Goldsworth Crimson' (left) is a cross between a hardy hybrid and *R. griffithianum* raised by W. C. Slocock Ltd in 1926. It received an Award of Merit in 1960 after trial at Wisley.

Bud   **   Flower **
Wood ***   Foliage ***
Flowering: mid-season

MARION STREET
'Marion Street' (above) was raised as a cross between 'Stanley Davies', an old red hybrid, and *R. yakushimanum* 'Koichiro Wada'. I was given three flowers by Francis Hanger, then the curator of the RHS's gardens at Wisley, and chose 'Stanley Davies' as one of the parents because of its good record as a parent of many fine hybrids – notably 'Britannia'. It was first exhibited at the RHS Rhododendron Show in 1978 where it won the Loder Challenge Cup for the best hybrid in the show, an immediate Award of Merit, and two other first prizes. The colour of the flowers, particularly at the half-open stage, is similar to 'Pink Pearl', which caused Fred Whitsey of the *Daily Telegraph* to comment: "a possible successor to 'Pink Pearl' for small gardens".

Bud   ****   Flower ****
Wood ****   Foliage ****
Flowering: mid-season

GOMER WATERER

'Gomer Waterer', raised by John Waterer, commemorates his son, F. Gomer Waterer, one of the great rhododendron hybridists. It was introduced at the turn of the Century. Although full parentage of 'Gomer Waterer' is not published, it owes its beauty to *R. griffithianum*, clearly showing the influence of the very old *R. catawabiense* hybrid, 'Madame Carvalho', as glamorised by *R. griffithianum*. The result in 'Gomer Waterer' is a large flower and truss, taller growth and a slight flush of pink in the opening buds, which fade to white when fully open. Further advantages are its late flowering, in late May or early June, thereby missing the late frosts, and in its immunity to the rhododendron fly.

The leaves are large and dark green, and the habit is very regular, making a well-formed bush up to 8ft (2.4m). 'Gomer Waterer' is a splendid plant as a specimen to stand on its own. AM 1906

Bud   ✳✳✳   Flower ✳✳✳
Wood ✳✳✳   Foliage ✳✳✳✳
Flowering: late

MRS FURNIVALL

'Mrs Furnivall' is another of those old hybrids raised by Anthony Waterer which were discovered growing in the old nursery at Knaphill when it was taken over by Gomer Waterer. It was rescued from the jungle of old plants, propagated and introduced by Gomer Waterer in about 1922. It is similar in colour to 'Mrs G. W. Leak' and at one time was thought to be a hybrid in the same series. However, 'Mrs Furnival' has different foliage and growth and lacks the glamour of 'Mrs G. W. Leak' with its impressive flare of red in the centre of the flower. Its one considerable advantage is that it is much hardier; it also makes a better specimen plant, being much stouter in growth. AM 1933. FCC 1948. AGM 1968.

Bud   ✳✳✳✳   Flower   ✳✳✳✳
Wood ✳✳✳✳   Foliage   ✳✳✳✳
Flowering: mid-season

SURREY HEATH

'Surrey Heath' is another hybrid from *R. yakushimanum* raised by John Waterer Sons and Crisp Ltd. of Bagshot. The other parent is the bright scarlet 'Britannia', but the resulting flower in 'Surrey Heath' is not as deep in colour as might be expected from this influence. It makes a very bushy plant but does not show the idumentum of *R. yakushimanum*.

Bud ****   Flower ****
Wood ****   Foliage ****
Flowering: mid-season

SOUVENIR DE Dr S. ENDTZ

Souvenir de Dr S. Endtz is one of the many attempts to improve on 'Pink Pearl'. It is a cross with that cultivar and an old red hybrid called 'John Walter' made by the Dutch nursery firm L. J. Endtz & Son. This has been partially successful in that the flower has a deeper colour and the habit of the plant is more compact. Something of the grace and size of the truss has been lost but it is a very good rhododendron in its own right and is probably better for smaller gardens than 'Pink Pearl'. AM 1924.

Bud ****   Flower ****
Wood ****   Foliage ****
Flowering: mid-season

MOUNT EVEREST

'Mount Everest' is described as a cross between *R. campanulatum* and *R. griffithianum*, and the influence of both parents can be seen clearly. The flower, for example, has a definite scent, although it seems to have inherited more hardiness from *R. campanulatum* than might have been expected. It is, undoubtedly, a very fine plant, making a well-furnished shrub of medium size, with good foliage. It flowers early, which makes it vulnerable to spring frost, but apart from that it is a hardy plant. It was raised by W. C. Slocock Ltd in 1930 and received an Award of Merit in 1953.

Bud ****   Flower **
Wood ****   Foliage ****
Flowering: early

IGTHAM YELLOW

'Igtham Yellow' is one of the best of the yellow rhododendrons, and has a large, interestingly shaped flower in good deep yellow. It was raised by G. Reuthe in 1952 from a cross between *R. decorum* and *R. wardii*. The same cross was made in 1951 by Lord Digby and given the name of 'Arthur Smith'.

Bud **   Flower **
Wood ***   Foliage ***
Flowering: mid-season

MOUNTAIN STAR

'Mountain Star' is another hybrid of my own that was raised from the pollen of three flowers given to me by Francis Hanger. I chose 'Mars' as one of the parents because it has an individual flower similar to that of *R. yakushimanum*. The object was to produce a similar shrub and flower, but with a deeper pink colour. This was only partially successful, and the colour is not as strong as I had hoped, although it has a glowing quality about it and looks particularly well in light woodland. The name was chosen following the guidelines in the rules for nomenclature to indicate the breeding – 'Mountain' for Mount Yakushima and 'Star' for 'Mars'.

Bud **** Flower ****
Wood **** Foliage ****
Flowering: mid-season

'STARFISH'

'Starfish' is one of several successful hybrids raised from 'Mrs E. C. Stirling' by Gomer Waterer of the Bagshot Nursery. It is a very distinctive plant with its star-shaped flowers and rich pink colour, but, unfortunately, it is not easy to propagate therefore has never become as widely distributed as its beauty deserves.

Bud   ****   Flower ****
Wood   ***   Foliage ****
Flowering: mid-season

'Purple Splendour' is a very distinct plant; there is nothing else quite like it among hardy hybrid rhododendrons. It is said to have been raised at the Knaphill nursery 'before 1900' and it is one of those that were re-discovered when the nursery was revived by Gomer Waterer in the early twenties.

Bud ****   Flower ****
Wood ****   Foliage ****
Flowering: mid-season

R. MACABEANUM

R. macabeanum is probably the most magnificent of all the large-leaved species. It will grow up to 45ft (13.7m) in the right conditions, and the leaves can be 18in (46cm) long and 8in (20cm) wide. The flowers also are impressive, and they are particularly interesting because of the pouches on the side that hold nectar.

R. macabeanum was discovered by Frank Kingdon Ward in 1928 in Manipur and received a First Class Certificate in 1937. It is, unfortunately, a tender plant, which needs ideal, frost-free conditions in a moist climate.

Bud *   Flower *
Wood *   Foliage *
Flowering: early

MOTHER OF PEARL

'Mother of Pearl' is a sport (one of the very few of any kind in rhododendrons) from 'Pink Pearl'. It is a particularly dangerous plant to have in a nursery because its foliage and habit are exactly the same as those of 'Pink Pearl' but the flower is different. It opens a pale pink and fades to pure white. A rather curious characteristic of 'Mother of Pearl' is that it has a faint but definite scent; this comes from the influence of *R. griffithianum*, in 'Pink Pearl', which itself has no scent. 'Mother of Pearl' also flowers a week or ten days later.

Bud **** Flower ****
Wood **** Foliage ****
Flowering: mid-season

PIERRE MOSER

'Pierre Moser', raised in 1914 by the famous French firm of Moser & Fils of Versailles, is an attractive and curious plant. Although it is a hybrid from *R. caucasicum*, it is a very tall grower; so tall that it is one of the few rhododendrons that needs regular pruning, about once in three years. It has an unusual flower, which is star-shaped and very pretty. It would be interesting to know the other parent, and it is probably more than a coincidence that 'Moser's Maroon', raised by Moser & Fils, is also very tall growing.

Bud ** Flower *
Wood **** Foliage ****
Flowering: early

MRS BETTY ROBERTSON

'Mrs Betty Robertson' is another near-yellow rhododendron raised by Peter Koster as a result of crossing 'Mrs Lindsay Smith' with *R. campylocarpum*. This particular named variety is distinguished as being the hardiest of them all, although it is difficult to account for this. It has red stems and good foliage of a roughish but not unattractive texture, and is a neat, compact grower, making a wide, spreading bush 6–8ft (1.8–2.4m) across. Its one weakness is that it is very prone to attacks of the rhododendron fly, so it is important to keep a watch for this.

Bud **** Flower ***
Wood **** Foliage ****
Flowering: mid-season

TORTOISESHELL

'Tortoiseshell' was raised in 1946 by Oliver Slocock, who selected several different clones, all of which are very attractive in their different ways. 'Tortoiseshell Champagne' is a tall-growing yellow, and is probably the hardiest of all of these selections. 'Tortoiseshell Orange' is deep orange, and 'Tortoiseshell Pale Orange', a plant of medium height, is in a lighter shade. 'Tortoiseshell Salome' has biscuit-coloured flowers shaded with pink, 'Tortoiseshell Scarlet' has bright orange flowers, and 'Tortoiseshell Wonder' is a salmon-pink of medium height.

Bud *** Flower ***
Wood *** Foliage ***
Flowering: late

CYNTHIA

'Cynthia', also once known as 'Lord Palmerston', is one of the best known of the older hybrids raised before 1870 by Standish & Noble in Berkshire. The flower, usually described as rosy-crimson, is somewhere between pink and red, and the colour is always deeper after a hard winter. The individual florets are large and are held in a big, well-formed truss. The published parentage, *R. catawbiense × R. griffithianum*, seems unlikely because of the deep colour of 'Cynthia'. It is a very hardy plant and is a cultivar that will grow well in any situation, given the one requirement of an acid soil. It certainly stands a position in full sun better than many that flower in mid-season. It makes a well-shaped, handsome bush up to 9ft (2.7m) high by as much wide under normal garden conditions. It has one fault – in the winter, from Christmas onward, the dark green leaves hang down no matter how mild the weather may be, and they do not revive again until the spring.

Bud **** Flower ****
Wood **** Foliage **
Flowering: mid-season

FRAGRANTISSIMUM

'Fragrantissimum' sounds as if it might be a species, but in fact it is a hybrid between *R. edgeworthii* and *R. formosum*, which received a First Class Certificate in 1868. Its chief feature is a delicious scent, probably better than in any other rhododendron. The only difficulty is that it is a tender plant usually needing greenhouse or conservatory treatment. Even so, several people have been able to grow it outside with some protection, often in tubs in the shelter of a porch. The foliage is particularly attractive, being dark green, heavily veined and shiny.

| Bud | * | Flower | * |
| Wood | * | Foliage | * |

Flowering: early

RACIL

'Racil' is a cross between *R. racemosum* and *R. ciliatum*, raised by E. S. Holland in 1937. Although many good small hybrids have been raised from *R. ciliatum*, it has to be admitted that 'Racil' is one of the less attractive, probably because of the considerable differences between the growth and flower of the two parents.

| Bud | *** | Flower | ** |
| Wood | ** | Foliage | ** |

Flowering: early

ALTACLARENSE

The name 'Altaclarense' is the latinized form of Highclere, the seat of the third Earl of Caernarvon in Hampshire, where the plant was raised. The plant is credited to J. R. Gowen who was, at one time, secretary of the RHS and helped and advised the third Earl to restore the garden at Highclere. A cross between *R. arboreum* and a hybrid between *R. catawbiense* and *R. ponticum*, 'Altaclarense' was introduced in 1831 and received a First Class Certificate in 1865. It has long since been superseded and it is doubtful if it is available commercially today. Even so, there are some magnificent old specimens in many parts of the country.

Bud ****   Flower ****
Wood ****   Foliage ****
Flowering: mid-season

MRS A. T. DE LA MARE

'Mrs A. T. de la Mare' has become increasingly popular as the result of the enthusiasm for flower arrangement. The colour, tersely described in the *International Rhododendron Register* as white with a green spot, is much admired by flower arrangers, as shown, for example, in their frequent use of the similarly coloured shell-flower (*Moluccella laevis*). But there is much more to 'Mrs A. T. de la Mare'. There is a translucent quality about the flower and the foliage, and although the leaves are often marred by being fasciated, this could well be an attractive quality for flower arrangers. It makes a wide, spreading plant, growing up to 6ft (1.8m) high by as much wide. Raised by C. B. van Nes of Holland, it is the result of a cross between 'Halopeanum' and an early hybrid from *R. fortunei* or even from a form of this species, to which it undoubtedly owes much of its charm, including an attractive scent. AM 1958. AGM 1968.

Bud ∗∗∗ Flower ∗∗∗∗
Wood ∗∗∗ Foliage ∗∗
Flowering : mid-season

LUSCOMBEI
'Luscombei' is a straight cross between the two species *R. fortunei* and *R. thomsonii*, and was raised in 1880 by T. Luscombe. It is not now widely grown but is a very attractive rhododendron with good foliage, which is halfway between the two parent species.

Bud ∗∗∗ Flower ∗∗∗
Wood ∗∗∗ Foliage ∗∗∗
Flowering : mid-season

CHINA A and CHINA B
'China', in its various forms, is a cross between *R. fortunei* and *R. wightii*. It is difficult now to trace the true 'A' and 'B' forms as plants available for sale. They all have strong growth and attractive foliage with large, deeply veined leaves. The colour of the flowers varies from pale cream to near yellow.
AM 1940 (1948 after trial).

Bud ∗∗∗ Flower ∗∗∗
Wood ∗∗∗∗ Foliage ∗∗∗∗
Flowering: mid-season

R. BARBATUM
R. barbatum was introduced, although it is not known by whom, in about 1849 from the Himalayas, where it grows at heights up to 12,000ft (3,660m). It is an interesting species in that there are small bristles on the stems. The flowers are a very startling red colour.

Bud ∗∗ Flower ∗
Wood ∗∗ Foliage ∗∗
Flowering: early

54

DIPHOLE PINK

'Diphole Pink' is one of my favourite rhododendrons, largely because of the distinctive quality of the colour. Its interesting, dark green foliage is slightly crinkled, which gives an attractive light and shade effect. It has a good habit, is late flowering and very hardy. Raised by Gomer Waterer of John Waterer, Sons & Crisp, it received an Award of Merit in 1916. It is said to have been bred from a hybrid giving the influence of *R. griffithianum*, but its extreme hardiness makes this seem unlikely, and there is no resemblance to this species in habit or foliage. The name is interesting. The original plant was growing for several years near a diphole in a stream in the Bagshot nursery and became known as the 'Diphole Pink'. It is, perhaps, confusing because some people think that it is a Latin word and call it 'Dyfoly Pink'.

Bud ✳✳✳✳   Flower ✳✳✳✳
Wood ✳✳✳✳   Foliage ✳✳✳✳
Flowering: late

P. J. MEZITT

'P. J. Mezitt' is a hybrid between *R. carolinianum* and *R. dauricum*, raised in the United States where it is much more widely planted than in this country. It deserves wider recognition here and is becoming increasingly popular. It is very early – March/April – but hardy because of the influence of *R. dauricum* which comes from Siberia. It has an erect habit and an additional attraction is the reddish bronze foliage. AM 1972.

Bud ****   Flower **
Wood ****   Foliage ***
Flowering: very early

LODERI KING GEORGE
This is a selection from the original 'Loderi' cross, *R. griffithianum* × *R. fortunei*. It has a pink bud, fading gradually to pure white, with the characteristic heavy scent of all the 'Loderi' hybrids. Many different forms of 'Loderi' have been selected and named, but there are few who could distinguish them independently from each other without the help of a labelled plant.

Bud **   Flower **
Wood **   Foliage **
Flowering: mid-season

GOLDSWORTH YELLOW
'Goldsworth Yellow' is one of the more successful hybrids raised from the yellow species *R. campylocarpum* by James Veitch & Sons in Surrey. It is said to be a cross between *R. campylocarpum* and 'Jacksonii'. The colour is a definite yellow and is enhanced by the flowers being pink in bud, which gives it a deeper tone. The habit is bushy and spreading, indicating 'Jacksonii' in the breeding. It will grow up to 8ft (2.4m). AM 1925.

Bud ***   Flower ****
Wood ****   Foliage ***
Flowering: mid-season

ELIZABETH HOBBIE
'Elizabeth Hobbie' is one of the many hybrids, raised by Dietrich Hobbie of West Germany, which are the result of crossing *R. forrestii* var *repens* with a number of hardy hybrids. The parentage of 'Elizabeth Hobbie' is *R. forrestii* var *repens* crossed with 'Essex Scarlet', a very old hardy hybrid that has a flower of a deeper and purer red than most of the hybrids of that period. The loose, straggly habit of 'Essex

Scarlet' is corrected in 'Elizabeth Hobbie' by the influence of the dwarf and compact *R. forrestii* var *repens*.

Bud ****   Flower ***
Wood ****   Foliage ****
Flowering: mid-season

BLUE PETER

'Blue Peter' may seem rather extravagantly named, because no rhododendron can really be said to have the clear, mid-blue colour of this maritime signalling flag. However, the wrinkled petals and the interesting pattern of the flower, lavender-blue with a lighter centre round a dark blotch, do suggest the effect of a stormy sea. 'Blue Peter' is a wide-spreading plant, with good, dark leaves, and grows to about 4–5ft (1.2–1.5m) high and 6–7ft (1.8–2.1m) wide. It was raised by Gomer Waterer in 1933 and has received the RHS Award of Merit.

Bud ★★★★ Flower ★★★★
Wood ★★★★ Foliage ★★★★
Flowering: mid-season

COUNTESS OF ATHLONE
'Countess of Athlone' is one of the few large-flowered mauve rhododendrons. For many years mauve was unfashionable, but now it is much more in demand and is found to be of considerable use in rhododendron plantings to achieve a balance of colour. 'Countess of Athlone' was raised by C. B. van Nes of Boskoop in 1923 as

a cross between
R. catawbiense 'Grandiflora' and 'Geoffrey Millais'. The object of this cross, no doubt, was to raise a large-flowered hybrid that would be hardy on the eastern seaboard of the United States.

Bud   ****   Flower ****
Wood   ****   Foliage ****
Flowering: mid-season

BEAUTY OF LITTLEWORTH
'Beauty of Littleworth' is one of the first hybrids from R. griffithianum raised by Alice Mangles of Surrey in 1900. It received a First Class Certificate in 1904, confirmed after trial at Wisley in 1953, which shows it has stood the test of time. The foliage is particularly good, being broad and dark green, but some of the lower leaves tend

to drop as the plants get older; a fault that can often be seen in other hybrids of *R. griffithianum*, particularly in the more vigorous tall growers like 'Beauty of Littleworth'.

Bud   **   Flower **
Wood **   Foliage *
Flowering: mid-season

BETTY WORMALD

'Betty Wormald' is one of the many rhododendrons raised to be an improvement on 'Pink Pearl', and it probably is. It is the result of a cross between a red hardy hybrid, raised by Peter Koster of Holland, and 'George Hardy', which is generally thought to have been one of the parents of 'Pink Pearl'. 'Betty Wormald' has a rather larger flower than 'Pink Pearl', and the truss is well built up. The colour is deeper, with a few spots in the throat of the flower, and the habit is better, being less inclined to grow tall and lanky and lose the lower leaves. 'Betty Wormald' could be described as rather flamboyant, but it lacks the individual charm of 'Pink Pearl'. AM 1935.

Bud **** Flower ****
Wood **** Foliage ****
Flowering: mid-season

R. RUBIGINOSUM

R. rubiginosum is distinguished by having been grown by the late Sir Frederick Stern in his garden at Goring on Sea, which was made in a chalk pit. Sir Frederick tried several of the Chinese rhododendrons that had been collected from areas where the soil was slightly alkaline. *R. rubiginosum* grew successfully for six years but later succumbed, although Sir Frederick thought this was due more to the dry situation in which it was growing than the effect of the lime.

Bud **** Flower ****
Wood **** Foliage ****
Flowering: mid-season

PINK PERFECTION

'Pink Perfection' was once widely grown and was often used as a substitute for 'Pink Pearl' when stocks of that variety ran out. Unfortunately, it is not as attractive as 'Pink Pearl', having a rather coarser colour with an undertone of mauve, and a conical truss, which is not as graceful as that of 'Pink Pearl'.

Bud ★★★ Flower ★★★★
Wood ★★★★ Foliage ★★★★
Flowering: mid-season

SUSAN

'Susan' was raised by a member of the Williams family of Caerhays in Cornwall, but introduced by W. C. Slocock. It was first called 'Williams campanulatum hybrid', probably to acknowledge the raiser while it was growing in the Slocock nursery. It is said to be a hybrid between *R. campanulatum* and *R. fortunei*, but there seems to be very little influence of *R. fortunei*, and it could almost be a very good form of *R. campanulatum*. The leaves are dark green with a brown underside and the plant has a neat habit of growth.
AM 1936. AGM 1938.
FCC 1954.

Bud ********   Flower ********
Wood ********   Foliage ********
Flowering: mid-season

ADMIRAL PIET HEIN

'Admiral Piet Hein' is an early hybrid from *R. griffithianum* and was raised by the Dutch firm of C. B. van Nes in about 1920. The cross is said to be 'Halopeanum' × 'Sir Charles Butler'. Raised originally by the Belgian nurseryman, Halope, in 1896, 'Halopeanum' is said to be synonymous with 'White Pearl', but this is somewhat doubtful. 'Sir Charles Butler' is a cross between *R. fortunei* and a hardy hybrid raised by George Paul, a nurseryman famous for the hybrid rose 'Paul's Scarlet Climber' and 'Paul's Double Scarlet Thorn'. The influence of *R. fortunei* on 'Admiral Piet Hein' can be seen in the slightly blue-coloured foliage and the texture of the flowers, which are also scented, although this could be from the influence of *R. griffithianum*.

Bud *******   Flower ********
Wood *******   Foliage *******
Flowering: mid-season

PRAECOX

'Praecox' is one of the best of the very early flowering rhododendrons to stand more frost than most. It comes out in February or March and its mauve flowers look particularly well with the daffodils. Raised by Isaac Davis of Ormskirk in about 1859, it is a cross between *R. ciliatum* and *R. dauricum*, no doubt inheriting its hardiness from *R. dauricum*. It was highly commended by the Royal Horticultural Society in 1861 and, received the Award of Garden Merit in 1926. The foliage, small, dark green and slightly sticky, is not as resilient as it might be and some of the leaves are inclined to drop in the winter.

Bud   ***   Flower ***
Wood ****   Foliage ***
Flowering: February/March

MRS T. H. LOWINSKY

'Mrs T. H. Lowinsky' is one of the most decorative rhododenrons. The shape and colour of the flower give the impression of an orchid. The foliage is dark green and the habit is excellent, making a well-shaped bush up to 8–9ft (2.4–2.7m) high and as much wide. It is difficult to believe the parentage quoted in the *International Rhododendron Register* as *R. griffithianum* × 'White Pearl', although this may be explained by the fact that it is said to have been raised by both A. Waterer and T. Lowinsky. But the general habit of the plant and its flower show nothing of the influence of the two quoted parents.

Bud   ****   Flower ****
Wood ****   Foliage ****
Flowering: late

SAPPHO

'Sappho' with its striking colouring is probably nearly as well known as 'Pink Pearl'. It is an old rhododendron raised at Knaphill some time before 1867 and is still very popular. It is a very tall grower – almost too tall because it is inclined to become straggly and unkempt. If left to grow into a big bush, however, it can be a very effective screen, although rather ungainly until it reaches maturity.

Bud   ****   Flower   ****
Wood   ****   Foliage   ****
Flowering: late

MRS CHARLES PEARSON

'Mrs Charles Pearson', a good hybrid raised by Peter Koster, is described as a cross between *R. catawbiense* 'Grandiflorum' and 'Coombe Royal'. The purpose of the cross was an attempt to find a hardier 'Pink Pearl', which would grow in northern climes. It was not entirely successful, but the plant produced is very attractive in its own way. It has been described as the Tired Businessman's rhododendron because the pale mauve colour with just a touch of pink, fading to white, looks particularly well in the evening light. It makes a well-formed shrub and has good dark green foliage. AM 1933. FCC 1955.

Bud   ****   Flower   ****
Wood   ****   Foliage   ****
Flowering: mid-season

R. PONTICUM

R. ponticum is a strong-growing, evergreen species introduced from Spain and Portugal in 1763. The foliage is dark green and lustrous with long narrow leaves. It will grow up to 15ft (4.6m) in a suitable soil and situation, and it is rather more tolerant of neutral soil than many others. It has become naturalized in some parts of the country and for this reason has become known as the common rhododendron. The flowers are predominantly mauve, but as all plants are raised from seed there can be many variations from near-pink to purple. It is not as hardy as might be expected, late young growth being liable to damage from early frosts, but this is overcome by its vigorous habit. It makes a good screening belt and can be clipped into a hedge immediately after flowering. It is widely used as a stock for grafting and any suckers should be removed when young or they will take over, smothering the cultivar.

R. ponticum is a rather controversial species, liked by some, reviled by others. The two different attitudes to it are illustrated by the following quotations:

From *Garden Design* by Sylvia Crowe:

Rhododendron ponticum looks its best in a shadowed woodland; in the sunlight it is unpleasantly insipid.

From *Trees and Shrubs in the British Isles* by W. J. Bean:

It is seen at its best in the open spots fully exposed to the sun, where it can take its natural form and spread in its own way.

Bud ***   Flower ****
Wood ***   Foliage ***
Flowering: mid-season

R. FULVUM

R. fulvum (top) is grown more for the beauty of its foliage than for its flowers. It has dark green, shiny leaves with a rich red felt underneath, which is even brighter on the young growth. Discovered by George Forrest in 1912, it received the Award of Merit in 1933.

Bud ***   Flower **
Wood ***   Foliage ***
Flowering: early

LAMPLIGHTER

'Lamplighter' (above) raised by Peter Koster in Holland, is a cross between 'Britannia' and 'Madame Fr. J. Chauvin', also raised by Peter Koster and is a hybrid from *R. fortunei*. 'Lamplighter' is useful because it grows tall without becoming leggy. The foliage is good, with long, green leaves. 'Lamplighter' received a First Class Certificate in 1955.

Bud ***   Flower ****
Wood **** Foliage ***
Flowering: mid-season

BODDAERTIANUM

'Boddaertianum', first introduced in 1863 under the name 'Croix d'Anvers', which was also known for many years as 'Bodartianum', was named after Boddaert, foreman to the famous Belgian nurseryman van Houtte of Ghent. It is said to be a cross between *R. campanulatum* and *R. arboreum*, but this is a little doubtful as it does not show much influence of *R. campanulatum*. It is a very strong-growing plant with handsome foliage. The russet-brown underside of the leaf and black spots in the centre of the flower are typical of some forms of *R. arboreum*. The growth is regular, making it a good specimen plant to grow in isolation.

Bud ** Flower **
Wood **** Foliage ****
Flowering: early

CURLEW

'Curlew' is a dwarf hybrid raised by Peter Cox of Glendoick, Perthshire, who considers it to be his best, if not the best of all, dwarf yellow hybrids. It is a cross between *R. ludlowii* and *R. fletcherianum* and received a First Class Certificate in 1969. Peter Cox advises in his book *Dwarf Rhododendrons* that it is better not to feed 'Curlew' too generously as it will grow out of character. The two parents are relatively new species; *R. fletcherianum* was discovered by Joseph Rock in Tibet in 1932 and *R. ludlowii* by the late F. Ludlow on one of his last expeditions to the Himalayas. AM (after trial) 1981.

Bud ** Flower **
Wood ** Foliage **
Flowering: mid-season

PRESIDENT ROOSEVELT

'President Roosevelt' is a hybrid about which very little is known; it is believed to have been raised in the United States and then put on the market by a Dutch nurseryman. It is a rhododendron which raises controversy. The connoisseur regards it as being rather vulgar and common with its bright gold, variegated foliage but in spite of this , or because of it, it is proving to be a very popular plant and will probably be seen around a lot more in the future when some of the problems of its propagation have been ironed out.

Bud   ***   Flower ***
Wood **   Foliage **
Flowering: mid-season

R. LUTESCENS

R. lutescens is rather a curious species because it differs from most other rhododendrons in not forming a truss. The flowers, which are funnel-shaped and of a good yellow colour, appear singly or in pairs. It was first discovered by Abbé David and introduced by E. H. Wilson in 1904.

Bud ✳✳ Flower ✳✳
Wood ✳✳ Foliage ✳✳
Flowering: early

LAVENDER GIRL

'Lavender Girl' is the result of a cross between the old hardy hybrid 'Lady Grey Egerton' and *R. fortunei*. 'Lady Grey Egerton' is a rather tall, straggly grower, and this has been corrected by the influence of *R. fortunei*, which has a much better habit. Similarly, the quality of the flower has been improved through the heavy texture of *R. fortunei*, but there is very little scent as with other hybrids from this species. This particular colour is now becoming much more popular, even if it is used only as a foil to other rhododendrons.

Bud ✳✳✳✳ Flower ✳✳✳✳
Wood ✳✳✳✳ Foliage ✳✳✳✳
Flowering: mid-season

LODER'S WHITE

'Loder's White' had something of a chequered career in its early days. It was raised by H. J. Mangles, but ended up with Sir Edmund Loder, who produced several young plants, which he passed on to friends. This ensured a wide distribution for 'Loder's White', which was unusual for a plant raised by an amateur. It received the AM in 1911 and AGM in 1931. However, it is not as hardy as these awards suggest and in a cold garden it needs a well-sheltered place. The foliage is apt to become damaged by frost and because the flower comes out early in the season, late April or early May, this too is often at risk.

Bud   ∗∗∗   Flower ∗∗
Wood ∗∗∗   Foliage ∗∗
Flowering: early

THE HONOURABLE JEAN-MARIE DE MONTAGUE

'The Honourable Jean-Marie de Montague' is something of a mystery; there are several different variations of the name, but the correct one should be 'The Honourable Miss Joyce Montague', which was the name given to the plant by C. B. van Nes in the Rhododendron Association's Yearbook of 1928 when this and many other new seedlings bred from *R. griffithianum* were put on the market in the United Kingdom. There is little doubt that, whatever the name, 'The Honourable Jean-Marie de Montague' is a startling red. The foliage is a good dark green, but the habit tends to be straggly.

Bud   ∗∗∗   Flower ∗∗
Wood ∗∗∗   Foliage ∗∗∗
Flowering: mid-season

HOLLANDIA

'Hollandia', raised by the Dutch firm of L. J. Endtz & Co, is a cross between 'Pink Pearl' and the very old *R. arboreum* hybrid 'Charles Dickens', and was an attempt to produce a deeper-coloured 'Pink Pearl'. 'Hollandia' makes a very well-shaped plant, wider rather than taller, and is like a deeper-coloured 'Cynthia'.

Bud   ****   Flower ****
Wood ****   Foliage ****
Flowering: mid-season

HYDON DAWN

This is probably the most spectacular rhododendron that has been raised for some years. The colour is striking and the size of the flower and truss is impressive, which is remarkable considering that it was bred from *R. yakushimanum*. If there is a criticism, it could be that 'Hydon Dawn' has lost many of the attractive characteristics of *R. yakushimanum*: the neat habit, the felted, rounded foliage, and the bell-shaped flowers. Even so, 'Hydon Dawn' is a splendid rhododendron and in the future will doubtless rival, if not surpass, 'Pink Pearl' in popularity. It was raised by A. F. George of Hydon nursery in Godalming, and the breeding is interesting, even surprising. It is *R. yakushimanum* crossed with 'Springbok', which itself is a hybrid between *R. ponticum* and *R. griersonianum*. AM 1985.

Bud	***	Flower	***
Wood	***	Foliage	***

Flowering: mid-season

AUGFAST

This is a somewhat ugly name for a very attractive plant – the result of an earlier fashion for naming hybrids with part of the names of both parents. The parents of 'Augfast' are *R. augustinii* and *R. fastigiatum*. They have produced a very attractive, small, rounded shrub, which carries many clear blue flowers. It is a suitable plant for the rock garden or the front of the rhododendron border, and is very free flowering.

Bud **** Flower **
Wood **** Foliage ***
Flowering: early

UNIQUE
'Unique' is one of the several cream and yellow rhododendrons raised at the Veitch nursery, Kingston-upon-Thames, and introduced by W. C. Slocock in 1934. It has a very neat, compact habit and attractive foliage, but the flower, being rather early, is liable to damage from spring frost. It received the Award of Merit in 1934 and a First Class Certificate in 1935.

Bud ** Flower **
Wood *** Foliage ***
Flowering: early

OLD PORT

'Old Port', raised by Anthony Waterer in about 1865, is another old Knaphill hybrid which has been grown for many years. The colour of the flower is well described by the name, the foliage and habit are excellent, and it is a plant with a remarkable constitution. I proved this with one big specimen plant, which went to five consecutive Chelsea Flower Shows, each time being re-planted and then lifted again the following autumn.

Bud **** Flower ****
Wood **** Foliage ****
Flowering: mid-season

KLUIS TRIUMPH

'Kluis Triumph' was raised by Anthony Kluis of Boskoop, Holland, during World War II. I introduced it in 1947, at the Chelsea Flower Show. It is a good red, with a shiny texture to the petal and an upstanding truss. The long, dark green foliage is good, and the habit is compact for a plant growing up to 6–7ft (1.8–2.1m). It was highly commended in the RHS's Rhododendron Trials at Wisley in 1968 and has proved to be a popular variety.

Bud **** Flower ****
Wood **** Foliage ****
Flowering: mid-season

YELLOW HAMMER

'Yellow Hammer' is a cross between *R. flavidum* and *R. sulfureum*, made at Caerhays, Cornwall, some time before 1931. It is a somewhat thin and straggly grower with rather sparse foliage, but it can almost be described as autumn flowering, so extensive is its second show of flowers. However, this cannot be relied upon, and, like other rhododendrons with this characteristic, any autumn flowers will be at the cost of those that would normally open the following spring.

Bud ** Flower **
Wood ** Foliage **
Flowering: early

LADY CLEMENTINE MITFORD

'Lady Clementine Mitford', raised by Anthony Waterer at the Knaphill nursery in around 1870, is a hybrid from *R. maximum* and shows many of its characteristics. The young growth, in the form of silver spears, is particularly attractive, and the fully developed foliage is also good, dark green and hanging down to cover the stems. The plant makes a very handsome shrub with good proportions. AM 1971.

Bud **** Flower ****
Wood **** Foliage ****
Flowering: late

BARONESS SCHROEDER

An early hybrid raised by John Waterer at Bagshot showing the influence of *R. arboreum* in the fine black spots in the centre of the flower. (There is also a Javonicum hybrid with the same name.)

Bud **** Flower ****
Wood **** Foliage ****
Flowering: late

CORONA

'Corona', which was raised by John Waterer of Bagshot and received an Award of Merit in 1911, is a very distinct cultivar, but it is very difficult even to make a guess at its parentage as there is nothing quite like 'Corona' among the older rhododendrons. It has a neat truss of many small flowers in an attractive shade of coral-pink, but probably its chief beauty is its proportion. The size of the plant, the flower, the leaf and the truss all seem to be exactly right.

Bud **** Flower ****
Wood **** Foliage ****
Flowering: mid-season

R. YAKUSHIMANUM

R. Yakushimanum is generally considered to be so distinctive and superior to all other rhododendrons that it is the general opinion of rhododendron buffs everywhere that no hybrid will ever be raised from it that is better than the original species. Something will always be lost, probably the most important characteristic of all, the beautiful proportions of the plant in all its aspects – shape, leaf, young growth and the very delicate form of the flowers.

It is slow growing and compact but by no means a 'dwarf', with the implication of an alpine plant. Left alone it will probably make a rounded bush up to 4 or 5ft (1.2 or 1.5m) with a slightly wider diameter. But at present established specimens suffer constant pruning for cuttings and scions because it is not easy to propagate yet very much in demand.

There are two forms in commerce: the First Class Certificate form which has now been given the clonal name of 'Koichiro Wada', and another known as 'Exbury Form' which has rather longer leaves with less indumentum, but has a deeper pink flower and holds its colour a little longer than that of *R. yakushimanum* 'Koichiro Wada'.

Bud ✳✳✳✳ Flower ✳✳✳✳
Wood ✳✳✳✳ Foliage ✳✳✳✳
Flowering: mid-season

ANNA ROSE WHITNEY

This is probably the most striking hardy hybrid to be introduced since World War II. Raised by W. E. Whitney of Washington, USA, it was the result of a cross between 'Countess of Derby' and *R. griersonianum*, and has inherited the best of both parents. It has the intensity of colour of *R. griersonianum* and has kept the good habit of 'Countess of Derby'. It makes a splendid shrub, tall and wide-spreading with good big leaves slightly yellowish-green in colour, which enhance the beauty of the flowers. Although it is rather prone to powdery mildew, the plant is so good that this is a risk worth taking. It has not yet received any awards, but it was only introduced in 1954 and has already begun to rival 'Pink Pearl' in popularity, which is sufficient recommendation in itself.

Bud ∗∗∗ Flower ∗∗∗
Wood ∗∗∗∗ Foliage ∗∗∗
Flowering: mid-season

CILPINENSE

The buds of 'Cilpinense' are a delicate shade of pink, which fades to pure white as the small, attractive flowers open. The plant's one disadvantage is that the flowers appear in March so are liable to be destroyed by frost. A favourite among connoisseurs, 'Cilpinense' has received many awards (AM 1927, FCC 1968, AGM 1968), and makes a neat, round bush about 3ft (0.9m) high and wide.

Bud ∗∗ Flower ∗
Wood ∗∗ Foliage ∗∗
Flowering: early

WINDSOR LAD

'Windsor Lad' is another of the hybrids found by Gomer Waterer still growing in the wild parts of the Knaphill nursery when he took it over in the 1920s. It is typical of many of the hybrids raised by the different Anthony Waterers of Knaphill – the characteristic, big yellow blotch. The name follows a line that was used at one time by Gomer Waterer to commemorate winners of the Derby.

Bud **** Flower ****
Wood **** Foliage ****
Flowering: late

ALICE

'Alice', one of the very early hybrids from *R. griffithianum*, was raised by John Waterer of the Bagshot nursery and introduced by his son, Gomer, who named it after his wife. It is a tall grower of somewhat thin habit in relation to its height but is a very attractive rhododendron. However, it has a rather volatile disposition. It will grow happily for many years and then suffer from a frost that leaves other rhododendrons unharmed, but it is so good that it is worth a place where it will receive some protection. As a matter of interest, when Gomer Waterer crossed 'Alice' with his own rhododendron, 'Gomer Waterer', he named the offspring 'Donald Waterer' which is the name of his son.

Bud ** Flower ***
Wood ** Foliage **
Flowering: mid-season

MARINUS KOSTER

'Marinus Koster' is very similar to 'Betty Wormald', which is understandable because it came out of the same seed pod. It is considerably more compact in habit than 'Betty Wormald' and is wide spreading. The flowers have a lighter centre, which also gives a different effect. AM 1937. FCC 1948.

Bud **** Flower ****
Wood *** Foliage ***
Flowering: mid-season

CUNNINGHAM'S WHITE
'Cunningham's White' is a very old rhododendron, raised as a cross between *R. caucasicum* and *R. ponticum* var *album* in 1850. It is a very hardy plant and at one time, before the Clean Air Act, it had the distinction of being the best rhododendron to grow in industrial areas. Even now there are many fine specimens in the streets of Birmingham. Now that it can be raised easily from cuttings, some growers are using it as a grafting stock in preference to *R. ponticum*, as they find that it does not sucker so easily.

Bud ✳✳✳✳ Flower ✳✳✳✳
Wood ✳✳✳✳ Foliage ✳✳✳✳
Flowering: mid-season

R. RACEMOSUM
R. racemosum is a good rock garden shrub with attractive red stems and flowers that are deep pink, almost red at first, fading as they mature. Discovered by Delavay in western China in 1889, it received a First Class Certificate in 1892. It is easy to raise from seed and there are consequently several different forms, the best of which is 'Forrest's Dwarf' (F19404), a good dwarf form with red branches and bright pink flowers originally collected by George Forrest and which has been propagated vegetatively.

Bud ✳✳✳ Flower ✳✳✳
Wood ✳✳✳ Foliage ✳✳✳
Flowering: early

DIANE

'Diane', raised by Peter Koster of Boskoop, Holland, is one of the many cream, yellow and near yellow plants resulting from crossing 'Mrs Lindsay Smith' with *R. campylocarpum*. 'Diane' has a surprisingly good habit considering that 'Mrs Lindsay Smith', is a straggly grower. It also has fine, dark green, glossy foliage, but this is liable to become chlorotic unless the plant is grown in some shade. It has a very attractive so-called yellow flower which shows up particularly well on the edge of dark woodland.

Bud ** Flower **
Wood *** Foliage *
Flowering: mid-season

DOC

'Doc' is one of the hybrids from *R. yakushimanum* raised by Messrs. John Waterer Sons and Crisp at Bagshot and named after the Seven Dwarfs. The other parent is 'Corona', creating a compact plant but with little indumentum on the underside of the leaves.

Bud **** Flower ****
Wood **** Foliage ****
Flowering: mid-season

R. YUNNANENSE

R. yunnanense is a tall, graceful, free-flowering rhododendron, which, although very hardy, is inclined to lose some of its leaves in the winter, particularly if it is in a rather exposed position. The colour is very variable and can be anything from white to mauve, clear pink, or purple. The flowers are almost invariably heavily spotted, which adds to its attraction. It was discovered by Abbé Delavay in Yunnan in 1889 and received the AM in 1903 and the AGM in 1934.

Bud **** Flower ****
Wood *** Foliage **
Flowering: mid-season

MICHAEL WATERER

'Michael Waterer' is recorded as a Ponticum hybrid raised before 1894. This could well be true because the foliage of the plant shows traces of *R. ponticum* but there must also be an influence from *R. arboreum* to give it the deep red colour. It was named after the original founder of the Knaphill nursery, which was started at about the end of the 18th century. 'Michael Waterer' is still a good rhododendron; a late-flowering red, which, although inclined to get straggly as a young plant, develops into a good specimen in time.

Bud **** Flower ****
Wood **** Foliage ****
Flowering: late

A. BEDFORD

'A. Bedford' is a tall-growing, very handsome shrub with dark green leaves and red stems. Raised by T. Lowinsky of Sunninghill, it is described as being a cross between a mauve seedling and *R. ponticum*. It has a good, large flower in a pleasant shade of mauve with a dark centre. There are not many in this colour combination and this is undoubtedly the best.

Bud ** Flower ***
Wood ** Foliage *
Flowering: late

NAOMI EARLY DAWN

'Naomi Early Dawn' was raised by Lionel de Rothschild. 'Naomi Early Dawn' is generally regarded as being one of his most successful hybrids, and there is no doubt that it is very beautiful, both in colour and in texture of petal. However, it is not to everyone's taste and my own view is that the truss is rather too lax, particularly as it becomes full blown unless the plant is growing in a sheltered position. It is the result of a cross between 'Aurora' and *R. fortunei*, and the parentage of 'Aurora' is 'Kewense' (which has the same breeding as 'Loderi') and *R. thomsonii*.

Bud *** Flower ***
Wood *** Foliage ***
Flowering: mid-season

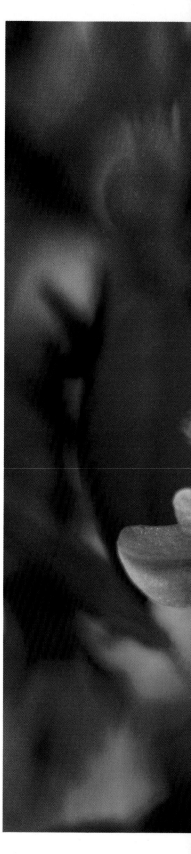

AVALANCHE

One of the many rhododendrons raised by Lionel de Rothschild in his garden at Exbury, 'Avalanche' (left) is a cross between *R. calophytum* and 'Loderi'. *R. calophytum* gives it the large leaves, which hang down and create a perfect dome shape when the plant reaches 20ft (6.1m). It is a tall, strong-growing rhododendron, carrying trusses of white flowers with just a touch of magenta at the base. It flowers in March, going on into April, which makes it vulnerable to spring frost.

Bud ****   Flower **
Wood ****   Foliage ***
Flowering: early

LADY CHAMBERLAIN

'Lady Chamberlain' (right) is a cross between the species *R. cinnabarinum roylei* and the hybrid 'Royal Flush', which is itself a cross between *R. cinnabarinum* and *R. maddenii*. This gives 'Lady Chamberlain' a considerable influence from *R. cinnabarinum*. The flowers are characteristic of this species: long, narrow trumpets, which hang down and look particularly beautiful when seen against the sunlight. The colour varies from salmon to orange suffused with rose-pink in different shades and tones. It is a tall-growing plant, with long, narrow leaves having something of the same appearance of a eucalyptus.

Bud *   Flower *
Wood *   Foliage *
Flowering: mid-season

SONATA

'Sonata' is a remarkable hybrid. Raised by G. Reuthe of Keston in Kent, he crossed 'Purple Splendour' with the orange-flowered species *R. dicroanthum*. The result is a very striking plant with orange flowers that have a deeper tone of maroon-red in them, showing the influence of 'Purple Splendour'.

Bud ****   Flower ****
Wood ****   Foliage ****
Flowering: mid-season

HYPERION

'Hyperion' is another old rhododendron which was rescued by Gomer Waterer when he took over the old family nursery at Knaphill. It was thought that 'Hyperion' would be an improvement on 'Sappho', for it has the same striking colouring but is a much less rampant grower with better habit and foliage. However, whilst 'Hyperion' is the better plant, 'Sappho' is far more popular, perhaps, because the flowers of 'Hyperion' are less flamboyant and slightly smaller.

Bud   ****   Flower ****
Wood ****   Foliage ****
Flowering: late

DR STOCKER

'Dr Stocker', raised by Mr North, might be described as one of the basic hybrids, being a cross between *R. caucasicum* and *R. griffithianum*. It seems possible that one of the yellow forms of *R. caucasicum* was used, possibly 'Cunningham's Sulphur', because 'Dr Stocker' has just the faintest hint of a cream colour in its flower. Also, one of the best yellows of all, 'Logan Damaris', was raised as a cross between *R. campylocarpum*, and 'Dr Stocker' and is a remarkably deep yellow for a hardy rhododendron. AM 1900.

Bud   **   Flower ***
Wood ****   Foliage ***
Flowering: mid-season

EARL OF DONOUGHMORE
'Earl of Donoughmore', raised by Dutch nurseryman Peter Koster and introduced in 1953, was the result of a cross between *R. griersonianum* and 'Mrs L. A. Dunnett'. It is one of the few successful hybrids from *R. griersonianum*, and has quite quickly become widely grown. The habit is rather curious, being somewhat branching and bushy, and almost forming a thicket. The growth is wiry and reasonably tough under normal circumstances.

Bud ✳✳✳   Flower ✳✳✳
Wood ✳✳   Foliage ✳✳
Flowering: mid-season

BLUE DIAMOND
'Blue Diamond', a dwarf rhododendron for the rock garden, was raised as a cross between *R. augustinii* and 'Intrifast' in 1935 by J. J. Crossfield in Hampshire. It is probably the best of this group of blue-flowered, compact dwarf plants.
AM 1935. FCC 1939.

Bud ✳✳✳   Flower ✳✳
Wood ✳✳✳✳   Foliage ✳✳✳
Flowering: early

ELIZABETH

'Elizabeth' is a cross between
R. griersonianum and
R. forrestii var *repens*. The
straggly, unkempt growth of
R. griersonianum has been
brought down into a more
compact form under the
influence of the dwarf-
growing *R. forrestii* var *repens*.
'Elizabeth' has a very striking
flower in clear scarlet. This is
one of the finest
rhododendrons raised at the
famous Bodnant Gardens by
the late Lord Aberconway.
AM 1939. FCC 1963.
AGM 1968.

Bud   **   Flower   *
Wood   **   Foliage   **
Flowering: early

TESSA

'Tessa' is a cross between *R. moupinense* and 'Praecox', made by J. B. Stevenson of Tower Court, Ascot, in 1935. It resembles 'Praecox', the well-known early-flowering cultivar, in its leaf, habit and shape of flower but it is considerably more attractive in its colour, being very close to pink. It also flowers more freely and, surprisingly, is more hardy.

Bud   ***   Flower ***
Wood **** Foliage ***
Flowering: early

R. RUSSATUM

R. russatum, one of the best of the dwarf rhododendrons, has aromatic leaves and deep purple flowers with a lighter centre. It was introduced in 1913 from north west Yunnan and received the AM in 1927, the FCC in 1933 and the AGM in 1938.

Bud   **** Flower ****
Wood **** Foliage ****
Flowering: early

R. ORBICULARE

R. orbiculare is grown as much for its foliage and habit as for its bell-shaped, rosy-pink flowers. It has heart-shaped leaves, which do not hang down but are held level with the ground. The bush reaches a height of about 8ft (2.4m) and is perfectly rounded. The young growth is also very attractive.

R. orbiculare was introduced by E. H. Wilson from western Szechuan in 1904. AM 1922.

Bud **   Flower **
Wood **   Foliage **
Flowering: early

PRINCESS ANNE

'Princess Anne' was raised by G. Reuthe of Keston in Kent and was originally named 'Golden Fleece'. It is a very attractive dwarf yellow plant, which is easy to propagate and is widely distributed by many garden centres. It is an unfortunate plant in one way because, like so many good rhododendrons, its normal flowering time is just in between the Royal Horticultural Society's Rhododendron Show and the Chelsea Flower Show. It was seen at Chelsea for the first time in 1986; the season that year was so late that 'Princess Anne' was out naturally at the right time for the show.

Bud **   Flower **
Wood ***   Foliage ***
Flowering: early

R. ARBOREUM

This is a variable species and there are many different forms. The specimen illustrated could be said to be about halfway in the colour range of red, pink and white, the best being a rich, almost blood-red crimson. The hardiness of the different forms varies in direct ratio to their colour; the deeper the colour, the more tender the plant. The foliage shown in the picture is also in the middle of the range; most forms have leaves with a silver underside, but some have a red-brown felt.

R. arboreum can really only be seen at its best in the milder parts of the United Kingdom where, in time, it will make a tree as much as 30ft (9.1m) wide and 45ft (13.7m) high.

Hardiness: variable
Flowering: early

MRS E. C. STIRLING

'Mrs E. C. Stirling' is a hybrid raised from *R. griffithianum* by Gomer Waterer of the Bagshot nursery. Its colour is a rather pale and washy pink, although the size of flower and truss is good. It was used as a parent by Gomer Waterer, who raised many other good rhododendrons from it which were distinguished by a flecked, pink colouring. These were very popular between the wars but they do not seem to be appreciated now so much and many of them have now gone out of cultivation.

Bud ∗∗∗　Flower ∗∗∗
Wood ∗∗　Foliage ∗∗
Flowering: mid-season

R. CAMPYLOCARPUM

For a long time a yellow rhododendron was as sought after as the black tulip, the blue rose and the red daffodil. *R. campylocarpum*, a good yellow species, was introduced from Sikkim by Sir Joseph Hooker in 1851 and received a First Class Certificate in 1892. Since then other yellow species have been discovered, notably *R. wardii*. Even so, one of the best yellows of all is still 'Logan Damaris', which came from *R. campylocarpum* crossed with 'Dr Stocker'. *R. campylocarpum*, a medium-sized grower, has delicate, cup-shaped flowers but does not flower until it is a mature plant.

Bud   **   Flower **
Wood **   Foliage **
Flowering: early

PINK PEARL

'Pink Pearl' is undoubtedly the best-known rhododendron. It is a very attractive plant, particularly at its half-open stage when the deep pink buds stand above the paler, fully open flowers. It was raised by John Waterer and introduced by his son, Gomer Waterer, in 1897, when it received an Award of Merit. It was given a First Class Certificate in 1900 and the Award of Garden Merit in 1952. The breeding is said to be 'Broughtonii' × 'George Hardy', but this is somewhat doubtful unless the hybrid 'Broughtonii' was different from the one grown in recent years in Great Britain, which is too early flowering to produce 'Pink Pearl'.

Bud   ***   Flower ****
Wood ****   Foliage ****
Flowering: mid-season

FRANK GALSWORTHY

This is an old hybrid and was raised in the Knaphill nursery some time before 1915 but not introduced until much later, when Gomer Waterer took over the nursery. The flower of 'Frank Galsworthy' is similar in colour to that of 'Baron Schroeder', and in some ways rather better, in that the purple has a stronger red tone and the yellow blotch is more prominent. Whenever 'Frank Galsworthy' is shown at the Chelsea Flower Show, it is always in considerable demand because of its attractive colouring, but it is very difficult to propagate either by grafting or from cuttings. Micro-propagation might be more successful, but would also be more expensive. It was named after Frank Galsworthy, the brother of John Galsworthy and well known as a flower painter specializing in camellias. AM 1960.

Bud **** Flower ****
Wood **** Foliage ****
Flowering: late

HARVEST MOON

'Harvest Moon' is another of the cream and near yellow plants raised by Peter Koster of Holland by crossing 'Mrs Lindsay Smith' (which he also raised) with *R. campylocarpum*. The red blotch is rather more prominent than might be expected, because it can be inherited only from *R. campylocarpum*, which has only a small red dot. AM 1948.

| Bud | **** | Flower | *** |
| Wood | **** | Foliage | **** |

Flowering: mid-season

GOLDSWORTH ORANGE

'Goldsworth Orange' was raised by Oliver Slocock in 1938 and received an Award of Merit in 1959. It made its international début at the Paris Floralies in 1964 as the centrepiece of the British exhibit, which won the second overall prize for the whole show. It caused a sensation at that show because it was then the only orange-flowered hardy rhododendron commercially available. Its colour is undoubtedly orange, even if somewhat pale, and it has a very handsome growth. The description of it in the *International Rhododendron Register* as low-growing does not, in my experience, seem very accurate. It is a straight cross between *R. dichroanthum* and *R. discolor* and has inherited the best of both species. It has the colour and the flower texture of *R. dichroanthum*, and the habit and late-flowering characteristic of *R. discolor*. Both plants have good petal texture.

| Bud | *** | Flower | **** |
| Wood | *** | Foliage | *** |

Flowering: late

EARL OF ATHLONE

'Earl of Athlone' has probably the most intense red colour of any of the older hardy hybrid rhododendrons. This could well be because one of its parents, 'Stanley Davis', raised by Davis of Ormskirk in 1890, is a particularly clear dark red without any trace of blue. The foliage of 'Earl of Athlone' is thick, heavy, veined and lined, which makes it an interesting plant when out of flower. However, it is a rather tender plant and does better in the milder parts of the country. It received a First Class Certificate in 1933 after trial at Exbury, a very mild garden near the Solent with high humidity, but it might not have achieved this high award had it been tried out at the Royal Horticultural Society's gardens at Wisley.

Bud ** Flower **
Wood *** Foliage ***
Flowering: early

CAROLINE DE ZOETE

'Caroline de Zoete' was raised by Arthur George of Hydon nurseries, Godalming, and it was very nearly destroyed. Mr George was having some ground cleared when he looked out of his office window and saw this fine flower on a plant among a batch of overgrown seedlings, which was next in line to be grabbed by the jaws of a bulldozer. He ran out and saved it, grew it on and it was highly commended in the Rhododendron Trials of 1985. It has heart-shaped leaves after the manner of *R. orbiculare*.

Bud *** Flower ***
Wood *** Foliage ***
Flowering: mid-season

MRS DAVIES EVANS

'Mrs Davies Evans' was raised by Anthony Waterer of the Knaphill nursery some time before 1915. It is a most attractive flower, with its fimbriated petals giving the impression of a double flower. The petals also have the advantage of making the flowers last longer because they give one another mutual support. Incidentally when rhododendrons were used frequently for the decoration of window boxes in London for the Festival of Britain, the Coronation and other events, it was found that 'Mrs Davies Evans' lasted in flower much longer than any other variety.

Bud   ***   Flower   ***
Wood   ****   Foliage   ****
Flowering: late

R. CAMPANULATUM

R. campanulatum is a rhododendron with a particularly neat habit and good foliage. It is also a large-flowered species with flowers very close to blue in the best forms but deepening to purple in others. There are also some forms with pink and white flowers, which are in their own way attractive. The leaves are dark green above with a rusty indumentum beneath. AM 1923 to a clone 'Knaphill' (lavender-blue). AM 1964 to a clone 'Roland Cooper' (white shaded mauve). AM 1965 to a clone 'Waxen Bell' (purple with darker spots).

Bud   ****   Flower ****
Wood ****   Foliage ****
Flowering: mid-season

R. DAURICUM

R. dauricum, one of the first rhododendrons to be grown in this country, was introduced from Dauria in south eastern Siberia in 1780. It grows up to 4–8ft (1.2–2.4m) and is a very hardy and early-flowering plant, often being in flower in January and February. For this reason, and because it has a similar rosy-pink flower, it has become known as the 'Siberian Mezereon', after *Daphne mezereum*. *R. dauricum* may not be a spectacular rhododendron, but flowering as it does in midwinter it is well worth a place where it can be protected from the worst weather, and also where it can be seen from the house.

Bud   ****   Flower **
Wood ****   Foliage **
Flowering: January/February

R. SUTCHUENENSE

R. sutchuenense is a species which was introduced from China by E. H. Wilson in 1901. It has pale lilac-pink flowers, and is a very beautiful foliage plant with large leaves, which hang down to cover the stems. It makes a big, well-rounded bush of considerable attraction throughout the year.

Bud   ***   Flower **
Wood ****   Foliage ****
Flowering: early

QUEEN WILHELMINA

'Queen Wilhelmina' is one of the hybrids raised from *R. griffithianum* by Otto Schultz in the greenhouses of the Royal Porcelain Factory in Berlin in about 1890. It was bought by C. B. van Nes of Holland, who made good use of it as a parent for 'Britannia' and other good hybrids. 'Queen Wilhelmina' passes on its glowing quality of colour and the almost gloxinia-shaped flower. Unfortunately, it is a somewhat tender plant and is only suitable for very mild gardens.

Bud   *   Flower *
Wood *   Foliage *
Flowering: mid-season

R. CAUCASICUM
Four of the *R. caucasicum* hybrids are shown here and overleaf as good examples of the progress that has been made by breeding from the original species. *R. caucasicum* itself is a scrub plant from the Caucasus mountains which seldom grows more than 3ft

(0.9m) high, and is now rare in cultivation. The hybrids take many different forms in various shades of pink, or occasionally yellow, but the two main characteristics of them all is that they are relatively early flowering, and they have a spot or blotch in the centre of the upper petal.

PRINCE CAMILLE DE ROHAN
'Prince Camille de Rohan' (left), raised by the Belgian Anverschafelt, was the first hybrid from *R. caucasicum* to be of good garden value with much better growth and larger deeper pink flowers.

Bud **** Flower ***
Wood **** Foliage ****
Flowering: early

CHEVALIER FELIX DE SAUVAGE
'Chevalier Felix de Sauvage' was the next improvement on *R. caucasicum* raised in about 1880. The colour is much

deeper than in 'Prince Camille de Rohan' and the leaves a little larger but the habit is similar.

Bud **** Flower ***
Wood **** Foliage ****
Flowering: mid-season

R. CAUCASICUM PICTUM
R. caucasicum 'Pictum',
(right), is a seedling form with
a more prominent blotch,
indicated by the word
'Pictum', and stronger
growth.

Bud **** Flower ****
Wood **** Foliage ****
Flowering: early

MRS G. W. LEAK
Raised by Peter Koster of the
Dutch nursery, M. Koster &
Son of Boskoop, 'Mrs G. W.
Leak' (below right) is a cross
between 'Chevalier Felix de
Sauvage' and one of the early
R. griffithianum hybrids, called
'Coombe Royal', which is no
longer cultivated. It is from
'Coombe Royal' that the
exceptional and striking
quality of the flower is
derived. 'Mrs G. W. Leak' is
probably one of the most
spectacular of all hardy
hybrids and is frequently a
prominent feature of the
Chelsea Flower Show as it
comes into flower more or less
naturally at that time.
However, this hybrid is rather
tender and particularly
vulnerable to spring frost.
Young plants can be killed
and the foliage of older plants
is often disfigured with dark
blotches, but the gradation of
colour in the flower is so
spectacular that the plant will
doubtless continue to be
grown for many years to
come.

Bud * Flower *
Wood * Foliage *
Flowering: mid-season

112

PROPAGATION

Rhododendrons can be propagated either by seed or by four vegetative methods: layering, grafting, cuttings and micro-propagation. Grafting requires considerable skill and knowledge, and micro-propagation is really only suitable for those needing large quantities of young plants. For the amateur gardener the best methods are by layering and cuttings.

Layering

For anyone who may need just one or two plants the old method of layering is probably still the best, as it needs very little equipment: a spade, a fork, a trowel and a few pegs. The method is to select a branch that can easily be bent down to the ground. It may be necessary to begin by bending the branch halfway and securing it to a stake so that the young wood can more easily be brought down to soil level. When the branch is in position, the ground where the layer is to be made should be prepared by digging and incorporating peat or leaf-mould and re-firming. If possible, the chosen branch should have two or three strong young shoots that can all be layered. The branch is then brought right down to a small hole, or nick, in the prepared soil. This nick should have a perpendicular back to it so that the young shoot to be layered can be bent into the nick with a right-angle bend. This is important because it will be at this bend that the new roots will form as a result of the sap being checked. The shoot is then well firmed down by

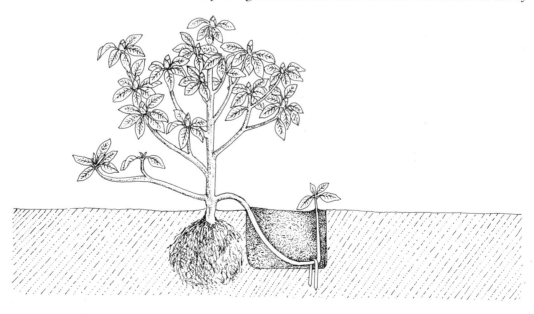

This diagram emphasizes the importance of a right-angled bend in the branch that is layered. It will be at this point that the roots will form.

pressing in the soil with the hands and further strengthened at the bend with either a wire or wooden peg.

The best time to do this work is in late summer or early autumn when the young growth has hardened off but is still supple. The layers should then be left for at least a year, preferably two. By that time they should have started to make good root and can be severed from the parent plant. They should be cut well above the soil at the beginning of August and then left undisturbed until the spring to enable them to draw root and start an independent existence. The following autumn they may be transplanted into a nursery bed of soil well mixed with peat or leaf-mould, and, if necessary, pruned after the second year, because layered plants are inclined to become leggy. They will then be ready for planting out in their permanent positions.

Grafting

Grafting on to stocks of *R. ponticum* used to be the chief way of propagating rhododendrons commercially, but only very enthusiastic amateurs used this method because of the work involved. The stocks have to be grown, which takes at least three years, they then have to be cared for, prepared and grafted, either in heated greenhouses or in cold frames with double glass, and the skill and knowledge required at this stage is considerable if there is to be a satisfactory take. However, this method may still have to be used for certain cultivars as there are one or two that will not strike easily from cuttings. Unfortunately, these include two of the best: the bright scarlet 'Britannia' and the best of all the species, *R. yakushimanum* 'Koichiro Wada', although it is probable that in time these will also be able to be grown from cuttings.

Cuttings

At one time it was thought to be almost impossible to grow hardy hybrid rhododendrons from cuttings, it was something of a propagator's dream. This has now become reality and will not only make them much more plentiful but also less expensive, because the overall costs are lower and the method does not require the highly skilled labour that was necessary for grafting.

At first, rhododendron cuttings were rooted in what was then the revolutionary method of creating artificial mist in a greenhouse with a very fine spray which was electronically controlled either by temperature or humidity. If the temperature dropped, or the atmosphere became dry, the mist would automatically be switched on to keep the cuttings turgid until they made root.

This was a great advance on the older methods of layering and grafting but it had certain disadvantages, not the least of which was to wean the young plants successfully from that atmosphere of intensive care. This is only mentioned as a matter of historic interest because there is now a new technique which basically only requires greenhouse conditions with a soil temperature of 70°F (21°C) and a light polythene cover for the cuttings.

The method that I am about to describe is one that I have used myself with success even under difficult conditions as, for instance, when the temperature controller went berserk and had to be switched off in the middle of a severe frost and the cuttings were frozen in their pans. Yet, surprisingly, this was one of the best takes we ever had although those conditions are not to be recommended

Rooting medium The medium for the cuttings is important. I use a straightforward mixture of two parts sphagnum moss peat, well broken down by hand but not sieved, to one part Silvaperl Perlite. Others find that a mixture of one part peat, one part Perlite and one part fine grade Cambark gives even better results, not necessarily in the number of cuttings rooted, but in the formation of roots in the later stages. Considerable care is

The side graft method used by the Dutch and taught to several English nurseries is to behead the stock, then to make a single straight diagonal cut, which should be as long as possible. Avoid twisting the knife to give any sort of minor kink or curve. As with saddle grafting, the scion is then selected to fit that stock, and a similar straight cut is made to match the cut on the stock. This operation is not easy, requiring considerable practice, training and skill.

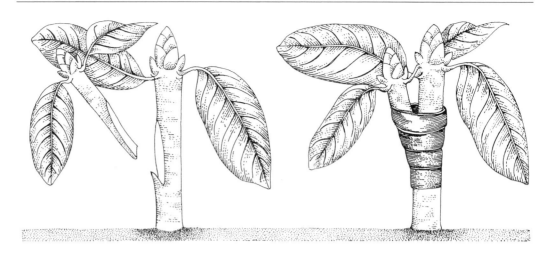

The saddle graft is the best form of grafting for rhododendrons. The scion should be fractionally larger than the stock to ensure that the cambium layers coincide exactly, the soft green tissue of the young growth being thicker than the hardened bark of the stock.

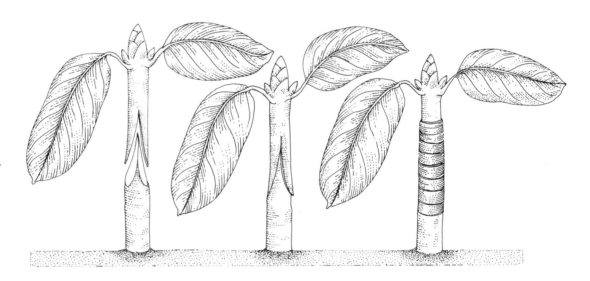

needed to ensure that the moisture content of the compost at the start is perfectly balanced. It should be moist but not wet, and just firm enough to hold the cuttings upright with no more pressure than being watered in with a fine rose. It is important not to firm the compost too hard and not to press the cuttings into it with a dibber.

Preparing the cuttings There is some discussion as to the best time to take rhododendron cuttings, but I find that I can start in September with the cultivars that grow out early and so harden off more quickly than others, for example, the 'Nobleanum' cultivars, 'Christmas Cheer' and 'Jacksonii'. As with all cuttings, a sharp knife is essential to give a good clean cut, and the stem of the cutting, excluding the leaves, which are left on the top, should be 2–3in (5–7.5cm) long. The cuttings should not be the strongest growth, but good healthy wood of medium or even small diameter, according to the cultivar. Wherever possible they should be taken from inside the bush or from the north side. Shoots that have formed flower buds should not be used. It is not necessary to have a heel of the old wood and the cutting should be complete, with its growth bud.

The cuttings should be prepared by having a few of the lower leaves removed, but they should not be stripped completely. The upper leaves that are left on the cuttings may

When preparing a cutting cut a piece 2–3 in (5–7.5 cm) long cleanly with a short cut horizontal to the line of growth. Trim off lower leaves and reduce the size of remainder, but do not cut them back more than half way. Wound by paring off a thin slice of the green outer bark on one side for about 1 in, (2·5 cm), as shown. Do not cut into the hard cambium layer.

be trimmed but no more than halfway along their length. This not only prevents transpiration but also makes it easier to put the cuttings into the trays. A small wound, about $\frac{1}{4}$in (6mm) long and only deep enough to expose the cambium, should be made on one side of the base of the cutting. When they have been prepared, the cuttings should be washed in a solution of Benomyl as a safeguard against the many fungal diseases that can attack unrooted cuttings; for the same reason absolute cleanliness of the greenhouse, the frame and all materials is essential.

Rooting auxins The use of rooting auxins (previously known as hormones) has been a strong contributory factor to the success of propagating rhododendron cuttings. There are many preparations used in the commercial production of rhododendrons, but these are not available to amateur gardeners in suitably small quantities. However, one proprietary product contains what has been found to be the most effective auxin for rhododendrons: Indol–3YL base utyrc acid. This is still known as Boots Hormone Rooting Powder. The active ingredient, utyrc acid, is used in several other ways, particularly by commercial growers, who have it prepared in a solution of acetone and water. It was then found there was some merit in this mixture as an aid to rooting. Accordingly, when using a powder such as Boots Hormone Rooting Powder, it is helpful to dip the cuttings in a 50/50 solution of acetone and water to make the powder stick to the stem. This should only be just enough to cover the $\frac{1}{4}$in (6mm) wound made in the cutting, which is now ready to be inserted into the rooting medium.

Propagating containers For convenience, the cuttings may be held in small, shallow containers, which should have adequate drainage with holes in the base covered by crocks to prevent them being clogged by the rooting medium. Better still are the Accelerated Propagation propagating trays where the cuttings can be put into their own individual pockets. These pockets are just large enough to allow the cuttings to make root, and they are open at the base, which gives good drainage and full advantage of the bottom heat. The AP propagating trays are now made in suitable sizes for private growers and should be available from many garden centres.

Heating The cuttings should then be placed in a propagating frame inside a greenhouse with undersoil heating controlled, preferably electronically, to give a constant temperature of 70°F (21°C). They should then be covered with very thin polythene (for small quantities the coverings used by dry cleaners are suitable), which, in my own experience, is better suspended above the cuttings so that it is touching only the tips of the leaves.

Another method is to drape it over the cuttings, although this is liable to cause disturbance when they need to be watered or inspected. Shading is important. Not only should the greenhouse be shaded but also the cuttings, using one of the proprietary nettings that give 50 per cent shade. This is then draped over the propagating frame on top of the polythene covering.

Rooting rhododendron cuttings in this way goes back to the old principle of propagation – warm below, cool above – so it is not necessary to heat the air in the greenhouse, only the soil holding the cuttings. Occasionally, for example, during an Indian summer, the increase in solar heat is so great that the temperature of the rooting medium will become dangerously high. Every precaution should then be taken to counteract this by giving plenty of air to the greenhouse, even providing an electric fan to help keep it cool, or a dual purpose fan heater, which can also keep the greenhouse frost free in very severe weather.

Aftercare Subsequent care and attention consists of removing the shading and the polythene for two or three hours in the morning on every third or fourth day. The polythene should then be shaken clear of the accumulated condensation, and the pans carefully examined for any dropped leaves or any rotted cuttings, which should be removed at once.

Each cultivar behaves differently but they should start to root within a month to six weeks, and, unfortunately, as they do not make a callous first, the only way to find out is by pulling out the occasional cutting to see if small white roots are beginning to form. As soon as this is seen to be happening, no further tests should be made and the cuttings should be left alone to make a good rootball. They should then be gradually hardened off by removing first the polythene, then the shading, and gradually reducing the temperature of the soil. If all has gone well, they should be fully exposed within the greenhouse by Christmas, and they may be potted up into 3in (7.5cm) pots from the middle of January onwards.

They should then be placed in a cold frame outside, protected with lights but not shaded. This has been found to be an important aspect of their subsequent development, but they will need shade from the beginning of April or the leaves and young growth will be at risk from burning as the sun gets stronger. As the cuttings develop, the shade should be gradually reduced so that they are completely hardened off for planting out in September.

Small-leaved rhododendrons Many of the small-leaved rhododendrons, both hybrids and species, may be rooted as summer cuttings while the wood is still flaccid but just hard enough to make it possible to cut out a cutting. A few may be rooted outside under handlights, using the same medium as for cuttings under polythene, and well shaded, preferably by the natural shade of trees. It is probably safer not to use rooting auxins for this type of cutting because they can be too strong and so cause the cutting to die back. The time to do this would be around the end of June or beginning of July, depending on the cultivar and on the season.

Seed

Hybrid rhododendrons cannot be raised from seed because of their long and complicated ancestry, and the results of random seed sowing would be unlikely to produce anything of any value. In theory, species rhododendrons should come true from seed but this only happens if they have been carefully prepared and then self-pollinated. Even then, the results can still be variable, and, sadly, one of the most variable of them all is *R. yakushimanum* 'Koichiro Wada', which is why there is so much speculation about its origin.

Nowadays, seed sowing will only be necessary when a deliberate cross has been made to produce a new hybrid. Depending on individual cultivars, the seed will be ready for harvesting at different times from October onwards, and should be collected when the pods are on the point of bursting. The pods are then allowed to ripen fully and open, when the seeds can then be shaken out. The best time for sowing is in April and the best medium is sphagnum moss (not to be confused with sphagnum moss peat, which, strangely enough, gives poor germination). If it is dry, the sphagnum moss may be rubbed down carefully through a $\frac{1}{4}$in (6mm) sieve, but if it is wet, it will have to be shredded by hand. Any containers may be used but they must be provided with good drainage. The shredded sphagnum moss must be firmed down well in the containers and watered during the process, and to ensure that it is thoroughly moist, it should be left for a day and then watered again. Sowing rhododendron seed needs a delicate touch because the seed is so small.

When the seeds have been sown, the containers should be covered with glass or polythene and shaded with newspaper. They can be placed anywhere reasonably warm, but not in direct sunlight, which would make them dry out. Heat is not necessary because they will even germinate quite happily in the open air, as they do where they have become naturalized. However, the American expert, David G. Leach, in his book *Rhododendrons of the World*, recommends starting them off with bottom heat of 75°F (25°C) to obtain quicker germination, which, with this help, will usually occur in about two weeks. As soon as the seedlings are large enough to handle, they may be pricked out into a growing-on medium of equal parts of peat, lime-free loam and sand or Perlite. They can be grown on under cover for a time but should be watched carefully for any sign of disease. Watering is crucial and they must never be allowed to dry out.

Micro-propagation

Micro-propagation, or tissue culture, is a new method of vegetative propagation, which was first used in Denmark to clean up carnations from virus diseases, and then later developed in France for orchids. It has now been used successfully for rhododendrons, particularly in Canada and the United States, but because the equipment required is very expensive and the work highly skilled, micro-propagation is really only suitable for large-scale production of thousands of plants.

The bare outlines of the method are that small pieces of the plant are placed in gels holding auxins to initiate roots. The gels are held in flasks, which are placed in growing rooms. When the pieces of plant start to proliferate, they can be divided and placed in different gels to promote roots. These can be divided again, giving an almost unlimited source of minute cuttings, which are then grown on in other gels to promote growth. The whole operation is carried out under laboratory conditions with very strict hygiene.

There are many advantages with micro-propagation: the plants will be clean from virus diseases, they will all be on their roots, and it seems so far that they tend to develop a bushier habit than by other methods of propagation. There is also the possibility that micro-propagation will induce sports, which are plants with different characteristics from the original, a classic example in rhododendrons being 'Mother of Pearl', a sport from 'Pink Pearl'.

AN ASIDE ON
NOMENCLATURE

Probably more than in any other plant, the social and political history of this country is reflected in the names of hardy hybrid rhododendrons. It is not so much that they are more significant than other plants but that they live longer and many of the older cultivars are still good garden plants.

Two of the oldest varieties, both of which are still in cultivation to a limited extent, by coincidence, have noble names – 'Caractacus' and 'Cetewayo'.

Rhododendron 'Caractacus' may have the oldest name of all, but it is unlikely that there was extensive breeding of hybrid rhododendrons in the first century AD. 'Caractacus' is a typical early hybrid showing the influence of both *R. arboreum* and *R. catawbiense*, and it was raised at the Knaphill Nursery in the middle of the 19th century. As every schoolboy knows (although this one didn't at the time), Caractacus was the name of a British chieftain who organized a rebellion against the Romans. (Even if it had been possible to breed and sell rhododendrons in those days, it was not a good name to choose – better to have called it after the Emperor Claudius who captured Caractacus and summarily carted him off to Rome.) But the subsequent story has a familiar ring. The Romans were so impressed with the bearing of Caractacus and his proud manner that the Emperor granted him a pardon.

Another old variety that is still quite widely grown is 'Cetewayo', a very dark, shining purple. Cetewayo himself was the King of the Zulus who, like Caractacus and the Romans, rebelled against the British, was captured and ultimately freed to return to become King of his people.

But for most of the 19th century new rhododendron hybrids were named after wealthy and influential customers or rather, more usually, after their wives to ensure a certain sale for a number of plants that would be sent to their friends and relations. This is why any contemporary catalogue of rhododendrons reads like Burke's *Peerage and Landed Gentry*, with extracts from the *Almanac de Gotha* when cultivars raised on the Continent are included.

Yet there were some curious breaks in this pattern which are difficult to explain. For example, who would name the best pink rhododendron of the period after an Italian motor car – 'Bianchi'? Yet this was the name of Gertrude Jekyll's favourite pink rhododendron, her favourite because the colour was more pure than most, with only a slight trace of the hairy heel of *R. catawbiense*, which gives the quality of hardiness to these early hybrids but detracts from the quality of the colour. All we know is that Gertrude Jekyll obtained her plants from her regular nurseryman, Maurice Young of Milford (of *Chamaecyparis lawsoniana* 'Milford Blue Jacket', etc.), but where he got them from is anyone's guess.

Likewise 'Amilcar', named after one of the first sports cars, with a cowl over the radiator to give it a racy appearance. The plant had an FCC in 1860 while 'Hamilcar', a similar 'Amanarth Red', went unrewarded.

This, of course, is not serious history – unless you happen to be interested in vintage motor cars – but there was a period, in the second half of the 19th century, when life was taken more seriously by the raisers of rhododendrons, and some were named after prominent politicians. 'W.E. Gladstone' or, as the plant is occasionally known, 'William Ewart Gladstone', is in two tones of pink and deeper pink; 'Sir Robert Peel' is crimson with dark spots. One raiser, probably the second Anthony Waterer, took especial interest in politics and national affairs about this time, for there are more names of influential men than before, and fewer duchesses, marchionesses, ladies and the like. 'Sidney Herbert', a carmine with dark spots, was named after the man who worked so hard for Florence Nightingale to be allowed to take her nurses to the Crimea, and she was equally honoured with her own rhododendron, a rose pink with a lighter centre. 'Charles Dickens' was the only Victorian man of letters to be so honoured.

The next great event was the Boer War, which is remembered among rhododendrons with the still popular 'Lord Roberts', a suitable military red with a dark blotch on the upper petal, symptomatic of the large moustaches favoured by the soldiers of those days. The 1914–18 war passed almost unnoticed until 'Armistice Day' was introduced by the Dutch, appropriately enough out of the same seed pod and in the same scarlet colour as 'Britannia'.

The inter-war years were marked with plants named after prominent European statesmen. 'Aristide Briant' was named after the French Prime Minister while 'G.T. Stresemann' was named after the prominent politician in the Weimar Republic in Germany who played an important part in the formation of the Locarno Pact. But somehow he lost his reputation in the eyes of the Dutch firm that raised the plant and it was later re-named 'Hollandia'. No British statesmen were similarly honoured, which prompts the question, 'Whatever happened to Lloyd George?'

The 1939–45 war is well documented in the annals of the rhododendron with 'Winston Churchill', although it has to be admitted that this is not a very good rhododendron, either in habit, colour or constitution. (But the great man's name is kept alive in many other flowers – a daffodil and a Michaelmas daisy being two of the best.) 'President Roosevelt' is a controversial plant with variegated foliage, reviled by some but loved by many. Like so many more, these were given names by the Dutch raisers who had an eye on their potential international markets. 'General Eisenhower', a strong growing red rhododendron, which has become popular, was better than 'Winston Churchill', but the United Kingdom's contribution to the successful outcome of the 1939–45 war was marked with 'Spitfire' and 'El Alamein', two good, late-flowering reds, both of Dutch origin.

This brings history as recorded in the names of rhododendrons more or less up to date, but it may well be the end. Plants named after personalities are not encouraged. If possible, they should give some indication of their origin. For example, I toed the line of the International Code of Nomenclature in 'Mountain Star', a cross between *R. yakushimanum* 'Koichiro Wada' (from Mount Yakushima in Japan) and the hybrid 'Mars' (named after a star).

A SELECTION OF SPECIES RHODODENDRONS

Awards made by the Royal Horticultural Society are indicated as follows: First Class Certificate – FCC, Award of Merit – AM, Award of Garden Merit – AGM; these are followed by the year in which the award was made.

The following two lists are selections of dwarf and taller-growing species, many of which have received awards.

Dwarf species giving good decorative value

Dwarf rhododendrons are particularly suitable for rock gardens, and some of them go well in the front of borders containing the larger-leaved kinds. They can also be useful in the heather garden because of their similar habit and their flowering period, which fills in between the winter and summer flowering heathers. Where the soil is alkaline, they are ideal for growing in raised peat beds in company with other small, lime-hating plants. The best way to treat most dwarf rhododendrons is to plant them in an open soil that is not too rich, and to mulch them well with peat or leaf-mould only, not rotted manure or artificial fertilizers. If put in the shade and well fed, they will grow loose and straggly.

It is sometimes difficult to define 'dwarf' exactly, as the height of a plant can often depend on the conditions in which it is grown. The following list includes some plants that grow to about 5ft (1.5m). All of them are decorative and relatively easy to grow.

R. calostrotum
The name, which means 'with a beautiful covering', refers to the hairs on the small, aromatic leaves. The deep purplish-red flowers, which appear in May, are flat and as much as 1–1½in (2.5–4cm) across, which is large in relation to the size of the plant. There is a particularly good red form called 'Gigha', which grew as a seedling in the famous garden made by Colonel Sir James Horlick on the island of Gigha off the west coast of Scotland. It flowers in May and June and has been awarded the Royal Horticultural Society's Award of Garden Merit. R. calostrotum was introduced in 1914 from north east Burma by Frank Kingdon Ward and George Forrest. AM 1935. FCC 1971.

R. chryseum
R. chryseum (the name means 'golden-yellow') is a very dwarf plant, with aromatic leaves, and small trusses of bright yellow, tubular flowers, which usually open in April. It has been used in hybridizing to raise some of the dwarf yellow hybrids. R. chryseum was introduced in 1912 from west China by Frank Kingdon Ward and George Forrest.

R. ciliatum
The name of this charming species means 'fringed', and it is not, strictly speaking, a dwarf plant. It becomes so only in less favourable gardens because of the effect of spring frosts cutting down the young growth. In mild climates, such as in Cornwall and the west coast of Scotland, it will grow as high as 9ft (2.7m). The flowers are elongated bells of a particularly attractive texture, and give the plant a delicate appearance. They fade to pure white when they are fully open, which is usually about the middle of March. To mitigate the damage from spring frosts, this species needs a position where it will be shaded from morning sun. R. ciliatum was introduced to Kew in 1850 from Sikkim. AM 1953.

R. dichroanthum

The name of this species means 'with two-coloured flowers'. There are several different forms of the species, of variable flowering capacity and in colours that can range from rich orange to pale pink. The best have orange flowers which are *hose-in-hose*, that is, with the appearance of having one flower inside another but not in the usual double form; this is because the exaggerated calyx looks like petals. *R. dichroanthum* grows to heights of 2–5ft (0.6–1.5m), and under suitable conditions spreads a little more than its height. The foliage is attractive, with long thin leaves covered underneath with a dusty grey indumentum, but seems to be prone to attacks of vine weevil. *R. dichroanthum* was introduced from Yunnan, China, by George Forrest in 1906. AM 1923.

An interesting and attractive species, *R. dichroanthum* has unfortunately never become widely available, largely because it is rather slow to flower and very slow growing. It has been much used by hybridizers for first and second generation crosses, and although many of these hybrids have been raised by amateurs and have only very limited distribution, there are some successful ones in fairly general cultivation. 'Goldsworth Orange' inherits a true orange colour and a large flower from *R. dichroanthum*, and strong growth from its other parent, *R. discolor*. 'Fabia', a cross with *R. griersonianum*, has light orange flowers and inherits the silver underside of the leaf from *R. dichroanthum*. 'Sonata', a cross between *R. dichroanthum* and the hybrid 'Purple Splendour', is a neat plant with good foliage, which bears little resemblance to either parent in its general habit except that the colour is unusual

in that it is deep orange, with no trace of purple from 'Purple Splendour'.

R. dichroanthum has also had an influence in secondary crossings, for example, through 'Goldsworth Orange', which, when crossed with *R. griersonianum*, produced 'Tortoiseshell'. There are several different forms of this hybrid: 'Tortoiseshell Champagne' (tall and yellow), 'Tortoiseshell Wonder' (salmon-pink), 'Tortoiseshell Scarlet' (bright orange), and 'Tortoiseshell Orange' (deep orange).

R. fastigiatum

This name, which means 'erect', is usually given to plants with tall close growth like that of a Lombardy poplar. It is a little difficult to understand why it was given to *R. fastigiatum* because this species is a dwarf plant suitable for the rock garden, usually growing to about 1ft (0.3m) high and as much across. It is covered in late April with mauve flowers, which vary in their intensity of colour, some forms being very close to blue. *R. fastigiatum* was introduced from Yunnan, China. AM 1914.

R. ferrugineum

This species is closely related to *R. hirsutum* and both are known as the 'Alpine Rose' and have the same characteristics. It is a dwarf plant with pink flowers, which appear in June, thus missing the worst of the spring frosts. The leaves are well described by the name, which means 'rusty-coloured', and the plant is not particularly decorative. However, it is an interesting plant historically because it was one of the first rhododendrons to be grown in the United Kingdom and, like *R. hirsutum*, it tolerates an alkaline soil. It was introduced from the Alps in 1752.

R. forrestii

R. forrestii has been used with the hardy hybrids to give new colours, particularly its own shade of intense scarlet. It is a variable species and the different forms can be either very good or very bad. Some of them are shy to flower, but the good ones have a brilliant scarlet colour with a shiny, waxy texture to the petals. The leaves are glossy dark green above and reddish-purple below. It is a plant for the rock garden or the peat bed, growing only a few inches high and spreading.

There is a form, now called *R. forrestii* var *repens*, which is even more close-growing and spreading. This too has started to have an influence on the hardy hybrids and probably the best known is 'Elizabeth'. It flowers early, usually at the end of April, which makes it vulnerable to spring frosts, and in cold gardens where these are the rule rather than the exception, 'Elizabeth' is seen in good flower only about once in seven years.

R. forrestii was named after George Forrest and introduced by him from Yunnan and Tibet in 1914. FCC 1935.

R. haematodes

This dwarf shrub usually grows to about 3–4ft (0.9–1.2m) high and as much wide. It is rather slow to set flower bud, so it does need a little patience. The small leaves are covered with a brown indumentum and, regrettably, are attractive to the vine weevil. The flowers have an exaggerated calyx, and are blood-red (hence the plant's name, which means 'blood-like') and are of a singularly glossy texture. *R. haematodes* was first discovered by Delavay on the Tali range, Yunnan, in 1885 and was introduced in 1911.

R. hippophaeoides

The name of this rhododendron means 'resembling *Hippophae rhamnoides*' (sea buckthorn) and refers to the foliage, which is grey-green and rather similar to that of the sea buckthorn. *R. hippophaeoides* will grow to 4–5ft (1.2–1.5m) or more in woodland but is usually grown in a rock garden. The flowers, carried in small trusses in April, are blue and near blue in shades of lilac and purple. This species is usually grown from seed, which can give considerable variation in different forms. A particularly good form, selected and grown on as a clone named 'Inshriach', has a deep lavender flower, which is darker at the edge. Other forms vary from not so good to bad, so it is wise to select plants in flower. *R. hippophaeoides* was introduced in 1913. AM 1927. AGM 1925.

R. hirsutum

R. hirsutum (which means 'hairy') is the oldest cultivated rhododendron, also known as the 'Alpine Rose' like *R. ferrungineum*. It grows on limestone formations in the Alps and will, consequently, grow on alkaline soils without artificial help. It is similar to *R. ferrugineum* and grows to about 3–4ft (0.9–1.2m) if left alone, but it is better planted in an exposed position where the weather will help to keep it more to its natural dwarf and bushy habit. However, leggy plants may be pruned as soon as they have flowered. A very hardy plant, it has flowers of a rather dull pink, which appear late, in June, thus keeping clear of spring frosts. *R. hirsutum* was introduced in 1656 but it is not known by whom.

R. impeditum

R. impeditum (which means 'tangled') is one of the blue dwarfs and is very similar to R. fastigiatum. It grows only to about 1ft (0.3m) in height with a tangled structure of twiggy branches, and is one of the dwarf rhododendrons that keep a neat habit. The flowers, which appear at the end of April or early in May, are lilac or mauve, near blue in the best forms. R. impeditum was introduced from western China by George Forrest in 1911. AM 1944.

R. keleticum

This species is very aptly described by its name, which means 'charming'. R. keleticum is a close-growing shrub, reaching a size of about 1ft (0.3m) high by as much wide, and has olive-green, aromatic leaves. The flowers are large for the size of the shrub and are wide, open saucers of deep maroon or purple. They do not appear until the end of May or June which helps it to avoid any late ground frost to which the plant would be exposed by its low habit. It was introduced by George Forrest in 1919 from Tibet. AM 1928.

R. leucaspis

This rhododendron is somewhat tender, growing only to about 18in (46cm) in height and width, but it is included because it is very attractive and worth a little trouble. The leaves, which are a particularly rich green, are covered with hairs, and the habit is slightly angular with drooping branches. The flowers are milk-white (hence the name, which means 'white shield'), and have brown stamens. They appear in February or March, and because of this the plant needs protection from frost when it is in flower. It was collected by Frank Kingdon Ward in Tibet in 1925. AM 1929. FCC 1924.

R. moupinense

Like R. leucaspis, this species is somewhat tender but is very beautiful and so worth some trouble. In cultivation it grows to about 2–3ft (0.6–0.9m) high and as much wide, and has dark green, rounded leaves. The flowers are in small trusses, and are usually white, although sometimes pink in the better forms. As with R. leucaspis, they have an ethereal quality about them, but because they appear in February and March they also need protection from frost. R. moupinense has been the parent of several very good dwarf rhododendrons. Named after the place where it was discovered, Moupin in western China, it was introduced by E.H. Wilson in 1909. AM 1914.

R. neriiflorum

This species almost grows out of the dwarf category up to about 4–5ft (1.2–1.5m). It is wide-spreading, and has leaves that are dark green above and white below. The name of the plant means 'with flowers like oleanders', and the flowers vary from deep pink to bright scarlet in the best forms, with a large calyx, giving them a hose-in-hose appearance. This species has been used with considerable success for hybridization with some of the larger-growing hybrids. There is a particularly good form of the species, now given the separate name of R. neriiflorum euchaites; this is a very distinguished plant, which has deep red flowers with a shining texture, and can grow up to 20ft (6.1m). R. neriiflorum was first discovered by Delavay in 1883 and introduced by George Forrest in 1906. AM 1929 to the form R. n. euchaites.

R. racemosum

The name, which means 'flowers in racemes', is only partly accurate; it describes the general pattern, but the flowers are not truly in racemes, like wistaria or laburnum. They are packed tightly down the branches, giving the effect of a raceme upside down. They are no less decorative for this and, as they are produced in a limited succession, they give a relatively long display compared with other dwarf rhododendrons. They are small, and open in April and May deep pink, almost red at first, fading as they mature. This species does not have a particularly dwarf habit and will grow as high as 6ft (1.8m) in good, shady conditions, but it is better kept down by pruning after it has flowered. It is a good rock garden shrub and the red stems add to its attraction.

R. racemosum was discovered by Abbé Delavay in western China in 1889 and it says something for its impact that it received a First Class Certificate in 1892. It is easy to raise from seed and there are consequently several different forms; the best being 'Forrest's Dwarf' (F19404), originally collected by George Forrest. This is a good dwarf form with red branches and bright pink flowers, which has been propagated vegetatively.

Illustrated on page 87.

R. russatum

R. russatum (which means 'reddened') is one of the best dwarf purple-flowered species, and, given time, will make a bush of 4ft (1.2m) in height. It has small, grey-green, aromatic leaves and flowers in shades of purple and violet, which appear at the end of April and in early May, making an attractive contrast with many of the dwarf yellow species and the dwarf narcissi. It was discovered in Yunnan by George Forrest. AM 1927 to a form with intense violet-blue flowers. FCC 1933 to another form with deep purple flowers. AGM 1938.

Illustrated on page 98.

R. saluenense

This is a dwarf shrub for the rock garden of somewhat variable habit, which is easy to grow in normal rhododendron conditions. The leaves are hairy, olive-green and aromatic. The flowers are broadly funnel shaped and usually rich magenta or purple. Its main flowering period is in April and May although, as with some similar species, it will occasionally give a second show of flower in the autumn. However, this will detract from the spring display the following year because no new flower buds will be set until the plant has made fresh growth. Named after the Salween river in Yunnan where it was discovered by Père Soulie, it was introduced by George Forrest in 1914. AM 1945 to a form with reddish-purple flowers.

R. scintillans

This is undoubtedly one of the prettiest, if not *the* prettiest, of all dwarf rhododendrons. The translation of the Latin name, 'sparkling', well describes the flower, whose small, prominent stamens do indeed give a sparkling effect. The flowers are blue or near blue, sometimes deeper, and appear towards the end of April or early May. It is hardy and easy to grow but, surprisingly, still not as widely planted as it might be. It was discovered by George Forrest in Yunnan in 1913. AM 1924 to a form with purplish-rose flowers. FCC 1934 to a form with lavender-blue flowers.

R. williamsianum

This species, named after J.C. Williams of Caerhays, Cornwall, is, in all but the mildest districts, a low-growing, ground-cover plant, because the young growth appears early and is often cut by spring frost. Even so, it is a valuable plant for its foliage, or as ground cover, because of the rounded, heart-shaped leaves, which are bronze at first and later turn to green. It is advisable to plant this species on rising ground where cold air can drain away in order to give it some protection from spring frosts during the danger period from mid-April to the end of May. In spite of its tenderness it has been used for some interesting new hybrids, which have mostly retained the cup-shaped flower and foliage of *R. williamsianum*, and have inherited hardiness from other species and hybrids. AM 1938 to a pink-flowered form.

Taller species giving good decorative value

The following is a selection of taller-growing species, ranging in height from about 6ft (1.8m) to anything up to 20–30ft (6.1–9.1m). They need the essentials of a moist but well-drained, acid soil, and shelter from cold winds. Their position needs to be carefully chosen because what often seems a sheltered spot can easily turn out to be a frost pocket. The best situation is a place on slightly rising ground, which allows the cold air to drain away, but with the natural shelter of light woodland. This also provides the right amount of dappled shade in which most of them thrive, silver birch being good companions.

They need to be planted with one eye on the artistic effect and the other on an appropriate selection. That is to say, it would be somewhat bizarre to place the large-leaved *R. falconeri* beside the willowy *R. lutescens* – some form of gradual arrangement, having regard to the character of the plants chosen, would be desirable.

R. aberconwayi

Named after Lord Aberconway, President of the RHS 1931–1953, this tall, rather narrow plant grows to 8ft (2.4m) and has dark green leaves that resemble those of an *Elaeagnus*. The flowers, which appear in May, are small, deep saucers and are white, sometimes with a touch of pink, with or without red spots. This species varies considerably when grown from seed and a selected form that has received the Award of Merit is 'His Lordship', which is white with crimson markings.

R. arboreum

Introduced in 1876, this is one of the most important species so far as the development of the hybrid rhododendron is concerned. There are many different forms, ranging in colour from rich, deep red to pink or white, with the deep-coloured forms being the most tender. The red forms of *R. arboreum*, crossed with hardier species to reduce its tenderness, have been responsible for all the early red hardy hybrids. As the name (which means 'tree-like') suggests, *R. arboreum* can grow to 30–40ft (9.1–12.2m) in height and width, but only in localities with mild climates.

AM 1964 to a clone 'Goat Fell' (cherry-red). AM 1968 to a clone 'Rubaiyat' (red with darker spots). FCC 1974 to a clone of *R. a. roseum* 'Tony Schilling'.

Illustrated on page 100.

R. argyrophyllum

This species is worth growing for its foliage and for the handsome form of a fully grown plant. It will make a big round shrub, anything from 6–20ft (1.8–6.1m), depending on the growing conditions. The leaves have a bright silver indumentum on the underside, hence the name, which means 'with silver leaves'. The flowers, which open in May, are usually white or white touched with pink, and are held in a loose truss of about 8 to 10, sometimes 16, individual florets. AM 1957 to the form *R. a.* 'Nankingense'.

R. augustinii

The best forms of this species are probably nearer to blue than any other rhododendron. Unfortunately, the best-coloured forms are the most tender. It is a tall-growing shrub for the woodland with narrow leaves, reaching anything between 4–10ft (1.2–3m), depending on the form and the conditions. The flowers, which usually appear in early to mid May are small and wide open, in different shades of pale lilac to deep blue with different markings. It is advisable to see the individual plant in flower before buying. *R. augustinii* was named after its discoverer, Augustine Henry (1859–1930), medical officer in Chinese Customs, later Professor of Forestry, Dublin, but was introduced to Europe from Szechuan by Frenchman Maurice de Vilmorin. AM 1926. AGM 1924.

R. auriculatum

R. auriculatum (which means 'eared') is a very tall plant, which looks ungainly in comparison with the average hardy hybrid, but it does have an elegance of its own. The leaves are long and light green, and the large, white, scented flowers are held in a loose truss, but are not seen until the plant has reached near maturity at something like 15–20ft (4.6–6.1m). The texture of the flowers is thin and they spot easily in the rain, but *R. auriculatum* is one of the latest-flowering rhododendrons of them all, opening in July and August. It needs a shaded situation and a moist but well-drained soil. It was introduced in 1900 from western Hupeh by Wilson. AM 1922.

R. barbatum

This is an interesting plant with good foliage and dark red, bristly stems, giving it the name *barbatum*, which means 'bearded'. It has rich red flowers, and a number of hybrids have been raised from it; the most surprising is one called 'Duchess of Portland', which, in spite of its parent's vivid red colour, is pure white. *R. barbatum*, which grows up to 30ft (10m) in ideal conditions, was introduced from the Himalayas in about 1849. AM 1954.

Illustrated on page 94.

R. bureavii

For the beauty of its foliage and young growth this species rivals the much renowned *R. yakushimanum* 'Koichiro Wada'. In the same way as that species, the young growth appears as silver spears, which later develop into thin, pointed leaves covered underneath with a thick, brown felt. The flowers, which appear at the end of May, are white or pale pink with crimson markings. It grows to 10ft (3m). Named after Edouard Bureau, a French professor, *R. bureavii* was discovered in 1886 by Abbé Delavay in Yunnan and introduced by George Forrest in 1908. AM 1939 as a flowering plant. AM 1972 for its foliage.

R. calophytum

R. calophytum (which means 'beautiful plant') is grown for the equal beauty of flower and foliage. It is a tall plant, which makes a well-shaped bush as high as 20ft (6.1m). The leaves, which hang down to cover the stems, are long and light green in colour. The flowers vary, according to the form, from white or pale pink to near pink, with a deep red blotch at the base. The truss is large and opens in early May, sometimes sooner, depending on the season. For a rhododendron with its lush appearance, it is remarkably hardy. It was discovered by Abbé David but collected by Wilson in Szechuan and Hupeh in 1904. AM 1920. FCC 1933.

R. campylocarpum

R. campylocarpum, which means 'with best fruit', has been the source of most of the best yellow hybrids. There were two forms at first: 'Hooker's variety', which grows to about 4–5ft (1.2–1.5m), and the variety 'Elatum', which will reach as much as 10ft (3m). However, it is doubtful if 'Hooker's Variety' is still obtainable. The rounded leaves are pointed at the tip, and are slightly glabrous over dark green. The yellow, cup-shaped flowers open at the end of April and are very delicate in their form, but they do not appear until the plant is reaching maturity. It is not an easy plant to grow and requires the best conditions. *R. campylocarpum* was introduced from Sikkim by Hooker in 1851. FCC 1892.

Illustrated on page 102.

R. dauricum

Named after Dauria in south eastern Siberia, this plant is known as the 'Siberian Mezereon' and has been grown in British gardens since 1780. It is only semi-evergreen and it makes a rather thin bush of about 4–5ft (1.2–1.5m), although some forms grow up to 7–8ft (2.1–2.4m). Like the Mezereon, the small flowers are pink–purple and appear in January and February. Although *R. dauricum* is very hardy, it is wise to plant it in a position shaded from the early morning sun so that the flowers last longer. AM to 'Midwinter', a good form with red-purple flowers, which is rather more evergreen than other seedlings.

Illustrated on page 108.

R. decorum

R. decorum (the name means 'ornamental') grows into a well-shaped bush of anything from 16–18ft (4.9–5.5m), depending on the form. The leaves are light green and faintly glaucous. The scented flowers, which appear in May and June, are of firm texture, usually white with a touch of pink, and a slightly stippled appearance. *R. decorum* was introduced in 1889. AM 1923.

R. discolor

The Latin name, meaning 'of various colours', is not very accurate because *R. discolor* can be grown from seed to produce a greater number of true plants than any other species. The reason is that it flowers late, in July, and there are few other rhododendrons in flower at that time, so there is little chance of cross-pollination by insects. The scented flowers are usually white, cream or pale pink, of a good quality and texture, and the leaves are long with something of a shiny iridescence. It usually grows up to 20ft (6m). *R. discolor* was introduced from China by Wilson in 1900. AM 1922.

R. falconeri

This species, with the impressively large leaves which distinguish several of the Himalayan rhododendrons, is not quite as difficult to grow as some of the others, but needs protection from the wind, which can damage the leaves. These are often as long as 12in (30cm) and as wide as 6in (15cm), and are heavily veined, dark green above and covered underneath with a rich brown indumentum. The flowers, opening in April, are either cream or pale yellow with a dark blotch at the base of the petal. In the wild the plant grows to 50ft (15.2m), but 25–30ft (7.6–9.1m) is more usual in good rhododendron conditions in the United Kingdom. *R. falconeri* was introduced from the Himalayas in 1850, and named after Hugh Falconer, Superintendent of the Saharanpur Gardens, India, in 1832. AM 1922.

R. fargesii

R. fargesii, named after Père Farges of the French Foreign Mission to Szechuan, is a species so free flowering that it can die in the effort; consequently, it is important to deadhead as soon as flowering is over. It grows up to 20ft (6.1m) but is more usually seen in the average garden around 8–10ft (2.4–3m). The leaves are dark green on top and glaucous underneath. The flowers are open cups, which vary from white to pink and are sometimes spotted. AM 1926. AM 1969 to a clone 'Budget Farthing' (white suffused with red-purple).

R. fictolacteum

This species has large leaves, which are dark green above and covered with a brown indumentum beneath, similar to those of *R. falconeri*. It can be grown with comparative ease in good average rhododendron conditions with some shade. The flowers, which appear in March and April, are white or blush-pink, with a dark crimson spot at the base. *R. fictolacteum* was discovered by Delavay in Yunnan in 1884. AM 1923. AM 1953 to a clone 'Cherry Tip' (white, pink-edged flowers with a deep crimson blotch).

R. fortunei

R. fortunei was named after Robert Fortune, who introduced the tea plant from China to India. *Like R. decorum* and *R. discolor*, *R. fortunei* has flowers of solid texture, which are also scented. The colour is not spectacular, ranging from white to pale pink with a suggestion of cream. *R. fortunei* has long, blue-green leaves, and makes a fine specimen plant 10–12ft (3–3.7m) in height and as much in width. It flowers in May, which means that it can easily become fertilized by any of the many rhododendrons in flower at that time. This has given rise to a warning in the Royal Horticultural Society's Rhododendron Handbook for 1980 that 'many plants in cultivation with this name are of hybrid origin'.

R. grande

This is one of the species that makes the rhododendron pre-eminent among the evergreen shrubs that may be grown outside in the British Isles. It grows to a tree or large bush (hence the name, meaning 'large'), up to a height of 30ft (9.1m), but it does need the very best conditions to do this: rich acid soil, mild moist climate, and freedom from spring frost. The leaves, over 12in (30cm) long and 6in (15cm) wide, are dark green and deeply veined while the undersides are brown overlaid with a thin film of silver. The flowers come in big trusses in March and April and are usually white with a very prominent orange stigma. It was discovered in Sikkim in 1849 by Sir Joseph Hooker. The species *R. sinogrande*, the Chinese version, is bigger and better in all its parts but a fraction more tender. Both should be planted out as young plants because, unlike almost all other rhododendrons, they dislike being transplanted when they are of any size.

R. griersonianum

R. griersonianum was named after R. Grierson, of the Chinese Maritime Customs, who was a friend and helper of George Forrest. It is a difficult plant to grow because the bright scarlet, somewhat papery flowers need shade, but its straggly, lank habit would only be encouraged by this condition. The long, thin leaves are not particularly attractive, but the buds are distinctive, with long sheaths, which cover them throughout the winter. The flowers, which open in June, are a vivid scarlet without any suggestion of blue. To a certain extent this species is continuous flowering, and also flowers well at a young stage although it is rather tender. It has been widely used in hybridization with only limited success, considering its advantages. It grows to about 10ft (3m).

R. griffithianum

This is a very tender rhododendron but one that is of considerable interest to the collector and the hybridist; it has probably contributed more to the quality of the modern hybrid than any other species. *R. griffithianum* has a very lovely flower, which is white just lightly touched with pink, and there is a faint but

definite scent. The immense flowers, as much as 6in (15cm) across, are carried in trusses of six or seven, and appear early in May. However, it grows with a rather loose habit and the branches tend to lose the lower leaves, which gives the plant a somewhat straggly appearance. It was introduced from Sikkim in 1849 by Sir Joseph Hooker, and was named after William Griffith, who was Superintendent of the Calcutta Botanic Garden, early in the 19th century. FCC 1866.

R. orbiculare

The name, which means 'circular', refers to the leaves but applies equally well to the habit, as the plant forms an almost perfectly rounded bush about 8ft (2.4m) high. It has interesting leaves, which are heart-shaped and silver-grey. The small, bell-shaped flowers are rosy-pink, a shade of deep pink that contains a strong element of purple. It is largely for its form and foliage that this species is grown. It is inclined to grow out rather early in the spring and is therefore tender as a young plant. The flowers, too, are susceptible to spring frost as they appear at the end of March or beginning of April. *R. orbiculare* was discovered by Wilson in Szechuan in 1904. AM 1922.

Illustrated on page 99.

R. rubiginosum

This species (the name means 'reddish-brown') is of particular interest because it offers a hope that it might one day be possible to breed a race of lime-tolerant rhododendrons. *R. rubiginosum* has been grown in a garden made in a chalk pit at Goring on Sea, Sussex, by Sir Frederick Stern. It has to be admitted that *R. rubiginosum* is not particularly attractive; its flowers appear in May, in clusters of four to seven, and are pinky-mauve, spotted with maroon on the upper side. But much could be done by breeding if that characteristic of lime tolerance could be developed. It grows to around 15ft (5m). *R. rubiginosum* was introduced by Abbé Delavay from south west China. AM 1960.

Illustrated on page 62.

R. sutchuenense

R. sutchuenense is a big plant with long leaves, and makes a handsome, evergreen shrub. It is hardier than many other Chinese species although the flowers, which are carried early in the year, in March, are liable to spring frost damage. The buds, however, are winter hardy, and expand into trusses of pale lilac-pink flowers with purple spots. The young growth, when it first appears, is covered in a grey bloom. *R. sutchuenense* was introduced by Wilson in 1901, and named after its place of discovery, Szechuan. AM 1978 to a clone 'Seventh Heaven' (flowers with a white throat, suffused with red-purple). AM 1945 to the variety *geraldii* (flowers with a deep purplish-crimson blotch). AM 1945 to a clone 'Sunte Rose' (red-purple in bud, opening with a red basal blotch).

Illustrated on page 109.

R. thomsonii

R. thomsonii was named after Thomas Thomson, superintendent of Calcutta Botanic Garden in 1854–61. It is a tall tree, as high as 20ft (6.1m), with distinctive orange-brown bark. The oval leaves are dark green on top and bluish-white below, making it a handsome plant when out of flower. The blood-red flowers are of rich texture and appear between April and May. They are best seen against the light although the plant itself grows better in woodland conditions.

R. triflorum

The name of this species, which means 'three-flowered', typifies many other species in the same series. They are all essentially woodland shrubs, with thin, tall growth, reaching as high as 10ft (3m). The flowers of the type are lemon-yellow, spotted with green and faintly scented. *R. triflorum* was discovered by Sir Joseph Hooker in Sikkim and Bhutan in 1849. A good form is *mahogani*, also known as 'Ward's Mahogany Triflorum', which has flowers with a mahogany-coloured blotch.

R. wardii

This yellow species has now had an influence on the yellow hybrids. It makes a well-shaped bush up to 8ft (2.4m) with neat leaves, which are green above and glaucous below. The flowers are cup-shaped and held in an elegant truss, opening in May. *R. wardii* was originally found in 1895 by Père Soulie but was introduced from Yunnan in 1913, by Frank Kingdon Ward, after whom it was named. AM 1926 as *R. croceum*. AM 1926 as *R. astrocalyx*. AM 1931 to KW 4170. AM 1959 to a clone 'Ellestree' (clear lemon-yellow flowers with a crimson blotch). AM 1963 to a clone 'Meadow Pond' (primrose-yellow flowers with a crimson blotch). AGM 1969.

R. wightii

This species was once thought to be tender but is now proving to be much more hardy. It forms a rather loose, tall shrub, up to 15ft (4.6m) high, with cream or pale yellow flowers in May, and thick leathery leaves, which are dark green on top with red-brown indumentum beneath. It is like a smaller edition of some of the large-leaved species such as *R. falconeri*. It has been used a little for hybridizing and one of the most successful hybrids is 'China'. *R. wightii* was discovered by Sir Joseph Hooker in Sikkim, and named after Robert Wight, 1796–1872, superintendent of Madras Botanic Garden. AM 1913.

R. yakushimanum

This incomparable species from the island of Yaku-shima in Japan could be described as the rhododendron of the future. The beauty of *R. yakushimanum* lies in its foliage even more than in its flowers. The leaves start as silver spears, which are then covered in a rich brown felt. Later they become rounded or ovate, dark green above and with that thick brown indumentum underneath. The fully formed leaves make a splendid background to the flowers, which are as simple as they are beautiful. Each individual floret is a shallow cup that starts out deep pink, almost red, and gradually fades through pink to white before it drops. There are hybrids from this species that have more colour, larger flowers, taller and stronger growth, and many other apparent advantages, but none of them compares with the charm of the simple beauty of *R. yakushimanum*.

The two plants introduced to England in 1932 are known as 'Exbury Form' and 'Koich-iro Wada' FCC.

Illustrated on page 83.

R. yunnanense

Although its general constitution is tough, this tall, thin shrub is inclined to lose its lower leaves in a hard winter, and is better seen in woodland. The flowers are open, attractively shaped with protruding stamens, and usually in colours varying from white to pale pink, spotted green or brown. There is a faint scent. Discovered in Yunnan, *R. yunnanense* was introduced to Paris in 1889 by Abbé Delavay. AM 1903. AGM 1934.

Illustrated on page 90.

SOCIETIES

Australia
Australian Rhododendron Society, Michael Dixon, P.O. Box 639, Burnie, Tasmania 7320, Australia.
International Rhododendron Union, Hon. Membership Secretary, c/o 67 Strabane Avenue, Box Hill North, Australia 3129.

Canada
Rhododendron Society of Canada, Dr H.G. Hedges, 4271 Lakeshore Road, Burlington, Ont. Canada.

Denmark
The Danish Chapter of the American Rhododendron Society Ole. Packendahl, Hejrebakken 3, DK 3500 Vaerloese, Denmark.

Germany
German Rhododendron Society, Dr L. Heft, Rhododendron-Park, 28 Bremen 17, Marcusalle 60, W. Germany.

Great Britain
The Rhododendron and Camellia Group of the RHS, Mrs Betty Jackson, 2 Essex Court, Temple, London EC4Y 9AP
The Scottish Chapter of the American Rhododendron Society, Edmund, A.T. Wright, Arduaine Gardens, Arduaine, By Oban, Argyll, Scotland.

Japan
Japanese Rhododendron Society, Teruo Takeuchi, 8–5, 2–chome Goshozuka, Takatsuk, Kawasaki, Japan.

New Zealand
New Zealand Rhododendron Association, P.O. Box 28, Palmerston North, New Zealand.
Dunedin Rhododendron Group, S.J. Grant, 25 Pollack St., Dunedin, New Zealand.

U.S.A.
The American Rhododendron Society, Mrs Fran Egan, Executive Secretary, 14635 S.W. Bull Mt. Rd., Tigard, OR 97223, USA.
The Rhododendron Species Foundation, P.O. Box 3798, Federal Way, WA 98003, USA.

Nurseries

Australia

Berna Park Nurseries, 5 Paul Street, Cheltenham, Adelaide

Boulter's Nurseries, Olinda Crescent, Olinda, 3788

Camellia Lodge Nursery, 348 Prince's Highway, Noble Park, Victoria 3171.

Cedar Lodge Creamery Road, Sulphur Creek, Tasmania 7321

P.& C. Deen & Sons, Monbulk Road, Kallista, 3791

Hilton Nursery, Hilton Road, Ferny Creek, Victoria

Lapoinya Rhododendron Gardens, Lapoinya Road, N.W. Tasmania

Olinda Nurseries, Coonara Road, Olinda, Victoria

Shrublands, 970 Mountain Highway, Boronia, Victoria 3155

Somerset Nursery & Garden Supplies, Bass Highway, N.W. Tasmania

Tanjenong Garden Centre (formerly Boults), Mt. Dandenong, Tourist Road, Olinda, Victoria.

Yamina Rare Plants, 24 Moores Road, Monbulk, Victoria 3793

Canada

Woodlands Nurseries, 2151 Camilla Road, Mississauga, Ontario 15A 2K1

Europe

6.D. Bohlje, Klamperesch, 2910 Westerstede, W. Germany

Joh. Bruns, 2903 Bad Zwischenahn, W. Germany

Firma C. Esveld, Baumschulen-Pepinieres, Boskoop, Holland

Hachman, J., Marken-Baumschulen, 2202 Barmstedt, in Holstein, Brunnenstr. 68, W. Germany

Hobbie, Dietrich G., Rhododendron Kulturen, 2911 Linswege, uber Westerstede, W. Germany

Jorgensen, Tue, Rijvej 10, DK 2830, Virum, Denmark

Nagle, Walter, Baumschulen, 7518 Bretten, Hotzenbaumofe 4, W. Germany

Seleger, Robert, Baumschule, im Grut, 8134 Adliswil, Switzerland

Wieting, Joh., BdB-Markenbaumschulen, Omorikastrake 6, Giebelhorst, 2910 Westerstede 1, W. Germany

Great Britain

Baronscourt Nurseries and Garden Centre, Abercorn Estates, Newtownstewart, Omagh, Co. Tyrone, N. Ireland BT78 4EZ

A. J. Clark, Leonardslee Gardens Nursery, Woodreeves, Mill Lane, Lower Beeding, Horsham, West Sussex

J. R. Clark, Lockengate, Bugle, St. Austell, Cornwall

Glendoick Gardens Ltd., Glencarse, Perth PH2 7NS, Scotland

Hillier & Sons Limited, Winchester, Hampshire

Hydon Nurseries Ltd., Clock Barn Lane, Hydon Heath, Nr. Godalming, Surrey GU8 4AZ

Knap Hill Nursery Ltd., Barrs Lane, Lower Knaphill, Woking, Surrey GU21 2JW

Millais Nurseries, Crosswater Farm, Churt, Farnham, Surrey

Reuthe Ltd., Crown Point Nursery, Ightham, Nr. Sevenoaks, Kent

Starborough Nursery, Starborough Road, Marsh Green, Edenbridge, Kent.

New Zealand

Alouette Nursery, Lauriston, No. 2 RD Ashburton, Canterbury

Blue Mountain Nurseries, Tapanui, West Otago

Boswell, Mrs E.D., 518 Hills Road, Christchurch 5

Campbell, Bruce W., 20A Waireka Street, Ravensbourne, Dunedin

Cross Hills Gardens, R.D. 54, Kimbolton

Jordan's Nursery, 6 Mekaube St, Ashburton

Opoho Nurseries, Mowat Street, Opoho, Dunedin

Riverwood Gardens, Main Road, Little River, Banks Peninsula, Canterbury

Rutland, Heaton, Stonebridge, South Canterbury

U.S.A.

Ace Garden Centre, 3820 Pacific Avenue, P.O. Box 306, Forest Grove, OR 97116

Azalea & Rhododendron Test Garden, 10408 Greenacres Drive, Silver Spring MD 20903

Benjamin Rhododendrons, 18402–A North Tapps Highway, Sumner WA 98390

Berryhill Nursery, Rt.4, Box 304, Sherwood, OR 97140

The Bovees, 1737 S.W. Coronado, Portland, OR 97219

T.E. Bowhan Nursery, 27194 Huey Lane, Eugene, OR 97401

Briarwood Gardens, 14 Gully Lane, E. Sandwich, MA 02537

Bull Valley Rhododendron Nursery, Rt.1, Box 134, Aspers, PA 17304

Carlson's Garden, Box 305–AR7, South Salem, NY 10590

V.O. Chambers Nursery, 26874 Ferguson Road, Junction City, OR 97448

County Gardens Nursery, Rt.2, Box 150, Mobile, AL 36609

The Cummins Garden, 22 Robertsville Road, Marlboro, NJ 07746

Dogwood Hills Nursery, Rt.3, Box 181, Franklyn, LA 70438

Eastern Plant Specialities, P.O. Box 40, Colonia, NJ 07067

Ellanhurst Gardens, Rt.3, Box 233-B, Sherwood, OR 97140

Farwell's 13040 Skyling Blvd., (Hwy 35) Woodside, CA 94062

Flora Lan Nursery, Rt.1, Box 357, Forest Grove, OR 97116

Frank James Nursery, 700 Pine Flat Road, Santa Cruz, CA 95060

Garden Valley Nursery, 12960 N.E. 181st, Bothell, WA 98011

The Greenery, 14450 N.E. 16th Place, Bellevue, WA 98007

Greer Gardens, 1280 Goodpasture Island Rd., Eugene, OR 97401

Hager Nurseries Inc., RFD 5, Box 641D, Spotsylvania, VA 22553

Stan & Dody Hall, 1280 Quince Drive, Junction City, OR 97448

James Harris Nursery, 538 Swanson Dr., Lawrenceville, GA 30245

Harstine Island Nursery, E.3021 Harstone Island North, Shelton, WA 98584

Hillhouse Nursery, Kresson-Gibbsboro Road, Marlton, NJ 08053

Holly Hills Inc., 1216 Hillside Road, Evansville, IND 47711

Horsley Rhododendron Nursery, 7441 Tracyton Blvd., N.W. Bremerton, WA 98310

Lawless Nursery, Rt. 3, Box 728, Beaverton, OR 97007

Mowbray Gardens, 3318 Mowbray Lane, Cincinnati, OH 45226

Roslyn Nursery, Dept.A., P.O. Box 69, Roslyn, NY 11576

Sonoma Horticultural Nursery, 3970 Azalea

Avenue, Sebastopol-, CA 95472

Stubbs Shrubs, 23225 Bosky Dell Lane, West Linn, OR 97068

Susquehanna Valley Hybrid Rhododendrons, Rt.4, Box 173–1, Millboro, DEL 19966

The Sweetbriar, P.O. Box 25, Woodinville, WA 98072

Transplant Nursery, Parkertown Road, Laronia, GA 30553

Trillium Lane Nursery, 18855 Trillium Lane, Fort Bragg, CA 95437

Verde Vista, RD 3, Box 3250, Spring Grove, PA 17362

Westgate Gardens Nursery, 751 Westgate Dr., Eureka, CA 95501

Whitney Gardens, P.O. Box F, Brinnon, WA 98320

Wileywood Nursery, 17414 Bothell Way, S.E. Bothell, WA 98011

GARDENS TO VISIT

Achamore House, Isle of Gigha, Argyllshire.
Bodnant, Tal-y-cafn, Denbighshire.
Borde Hill, Haywards Heath, Sussex.
Brodick Castle, Brodick, Isle of Arran, Buteshire.
Burncoose Gardens, Gwennap, Redruth, Cornwall.
Coles, Privett, Hampshire.
Dawyck House, Stobo, Peeblesshire.
Edinburgh Botanic Gardens, off Ferry Road, Edinburgh.
Exbury, near Southampton, Hampshire.
Glenarn, Rhu, Dumbartonshire.
The Hirsel (Dundock Wood), Coldstream, Berwickshire.

Holker Hall, Cark in Cartmel, Lancashire.
Inverewe, Poolewe, Wester Ross.
Isabella Plantation, Richmond Park, Richmond, Surrey.
Kew Gardens, Kew, Surrey.
Leonardslee, Lower Beeding, Sussex.
Lochinch, Castle Kennedy, Wigtownshire.
Logan, Ardwell, Wigtownshire.
Minterne, Minterne Magna, Cerne Abbas, Dorset.
Muncaster Castle, Ravenglass, Cumberland.
Nymans, Handcross, Sussex.
Penjerrick, Budock Water, Cornwall.
Portmeiron, Portmadoc, Caernarvonshire.

Powis Castle, Welshpool, Montgomery.
Sandling Park, Hythe, Kent.
Savill Garden, Windsor Great Park, Berkshire.
Sheffield Park, Fletching, Sussex.
South Lodge, Lower Beeding, Sussex.
Stourhead, Mere, Wiltshire.
Trewithen, Grampound, Cornwall.
Valley Garden, Harrogate, Yorkshire.
Wakehurst Place, Ardingly, Sussex.
Waterhouse Plantations, Bushy Park, Middlesex.
Wisley Gardens, Ripley, Surrey.

GLOSSARY

Auxin This is a substance to promote the growth of roots, previously called a hormone.

Bud (growth) The latent tip of the growing shoot from which the following year's growth and flower will develop.

Bud (flower) The dormant flower sheathed in leaves usually formed in late summer and clearly visible throughout the winter.

Callus The 'scab' of plant tissue which develops over a wound and, in grafting, joins the scion to the stock.

Calyx The outer shield of the flower, sometimes a petal or a leaf or an amalgam of the two.

Cambium A layer of plant tissue between the wood and the outer bark.

Clones Clones are selected forms of a species that are given clonal names; a good example is the claret-coloured form of *R. calostrotum*. This was first known as *R. calostrotum* 'Red Form' but is now called *R. calostrotum* 'Gigha', after Sir James Horlick's garden on the Isle of Gigha, where it occurred as a seedling. A clonal selection of this kind has to be subsequently reproduced by vegetative propagation as it would not come true from seed. Clones also come into the nomenclature of hybrids.

Cultivar A new word for 'variety', indicating any plant that has been raised which is different from the parent species and deemed worthy of a distinct name. In rhododendrons this could be a selected form of a species, a hybrid or a sport, all of which need to be propagated by vegetative means from the original plant or others grown from it in the same way. (Note: This somewhat clumsy word for 'variety' was adopted by the International Commission for the Nomenclature of Cultivated Plants as being more universally explicit than the many different national terms – e.g., 'variety' (English), *variété* (French), *sorte* (German), *sort* (Scandinavian languages and Russian), *ras* or *varietit* (Dutch), *razza* (Italian).)

Forms These are variations of species that are sufficiently different, either as the result of natural causes or the change in environment from a natural to a cultivated habitat, to be distinguished from the main species by name. If they are different enough and at the same time an improvement on the normal (the type plant, as it is called), they are selected as *clones*.

Glaucous Glaucous (or, sometimes, glabrous) means with a grey or silver sheen to the leaf, either shiny or matt, or even just plain grey.

Hybrids A hybrid is defined as a plant raised by crossing two species, although it can equally well be a cross between two hybrids, or a hybrid and a species. With rhododendrons the same cross can be made by different people, or even by the same person, and can quite often have different results. The cross is known as a *grex*; an individual seedling selected from that cross would then be a *clone*, to be given a separate name and to be perpetuated by vegetative propagation. A good example is 'Tortoiseshell', raised by Oliver Slocock. The grex is a cross between 'Goldsworth Orange' and *R. griersonianum*, and clones that have been selected and named are 'Tortoiseshell Salome',

'Tortoiseshell Wonder', 'Tortoiseshell Champagne', and 'Tortoiseshell Orange'.

Indumentum   This describes any light covering of the leaf, usually in the form of very fine hairs. In rhododendrons this is more often to be seen on the underside, giving an attractive contrast when the leaves are moved by the wind.

Scion   This is a short length of young wood cut to graft on to a stock to increase desirable cultivars.

Species   Technically, a species is a group of individual plants that have the same constant and distinctive characters. This means that, in theory, a true species can be reproduced from seed and those constant and distinctive characters will be inherited by the seedlings, provided there has been no natural cross-pollination by insects. Furthermore, it should also mean that the plants will all be the same wherever they may be found in the wild. But with the *Rhododendron* genus, this is not so. There are variations caused by different conditions of soil and climate. For example, the plant that grows on a mountain will vary considerably with the altitude. For this and other reasons species are sometimes subdivided into *forms*.

Sport   A sport is a branch or shoot which grows from the plant having different characteristics. The classic example is 'Mother of Pearl', a sport from 'Pink Pearl', which is white, later to flower and slightly fragrant.

Stock   A young plant of common, easily grown species, grown specially to support a more desirable species or cultivar by the process of grafting. Usually *R. ponticum* for rhododendrons.

Truss   This is the complete flower of the rhododendron made up of several individual florets to form an inverted cornucopia of colour. The formation of the truss varies considerably in different species and cultivars and is an important factor in their overall presentation.

Typography   Species are printed in italics with the initial letter in lower case – when hand written or typed the name should be underlined. Cultivars of all kinds – hybrids, sports, selected forms, are printed in roman letters and in single quotation marks, e.g., 'Pink Pearl'.

Vegetative propagation   This describes any means of reproducing plants other than from seed. These include cuttings, layering, grafting, in-arching and micropropagation (or tissue culture).

RECOMMENDED VARIETIES

The following lists of rhododendrons have been chosen for the various categories but they are not all necessarily illustrated or described in full in the text.

Tall Growing Rhododendrons

Species
R. auriculatum white
R. falconeri creamy-white
R. ponticum mauve
R. thomsonii blood-red

Hybrids
A. Bedford mauve
Avalanche white-flushed pink
General Eisenhower red
Hyperion white, chocolate blotch
Lamplighter light red
Loderi pink/white
Mrs T. H. Lowinsky white, orange blotch
Sappho white, black spot

Medium Growing Rhododendrons

Species
R. bureavii variable white to mauve
R. campylocarpum yellow
R. decorum white flushed pink
R. orbiculare rosy-pink

Hybrids
Betty Wormald pink
Cynthia rosy-crimson
Diane light yellow

Diphole Pink pink
Goldsworth Yellow apricot-yellow
Kluis Sensation pink, yellow blotch
Kluis Triumph red
Lady Clementine Mitford pink, yellow centre
Mrs Furnivall light pink, red centre
Madame de Bruin bright red
Mrs A. T. de la Mare white
Old Port deep red
Purple Splendour purple
Susan lavender

Bushy Compact Growers

Species
R. dichroanthum orange/pink
R. haematodes blood-red
R. neriiflorum deep pink to bright scarlet
R. smirnowii rosy-purple
R. souliei soft rose
R. wardii yellow
R. yakushimanum pink buds opening to white

Hybrids
Blue Peter lavender/blue, dark blotch
Britannia scarlet
Chevalier Felix de Sauvage deep pink
Corona pink
Doc light pink
Goldsworth Orange orange
Helen Schiffner white
Hydon Glow rich pink
Marion Street pink

Mountain Star pink, light centre
Percy Wiseman creamy-pink
Surrey Heath red, white centre
Unique cream/yellow
Wilgens Ruby dark red

Rhododendrons Suitable for the Rock Garden

Species
R. ciliatum white
R. fastigiatum mauve/blue
R. ferrugineum pink
R. forrestii var. repens scarlet
R. haematodes blood-red
R. hirsutum dull pink
R. impeditum lilac/blue
R. keleticum maroon/purple
R. leucaspis white
R. pemakoense pink-purple
R. racemosum pink
R. radicans purple
R. russatum purple
R. williamsianum pink

Hybrids
Augfast blue
Blue Diamond blue
Blue Peter lavender/blue
Bow Bells rose-pink
Cilpinense white
Curlew yellow
Elizabeth scarlet
Elizabeth Hobbie red
Pink Drift rose-pink
Princess Anne yellow
Rosy Bell soft pink
Sapphire blue
Temple Belle rich rose

Early Flowering Rhododendrons

Species
R. arboreum red to white
R. barbatum crimson-scarlet
R. ciliatum white
R. dauricum rosy-pink
R. mucronulatum pale purple/rose
R. thomsonii blood-red

Hybrids
Christmas Cheer pale pink
Cilpinense white
Jacksonii pink
Nobleanum forms
P. J. Mezitt deep pink
Praecox mauve
Racil blush
Rosamundii light pink

Mid-season Rhododendrons

Species
R. aberconwayi white-tinged pink
R. augustinii blue
R. decorum white-flushed pink
R. fargesii rose-pink
R. fortunei pink to white
R. neriiflorum deep pink to bright scarlet

Hybrids
Anna Rose Whitney bright red
Betty Wormald pink
Countess of Athlone mauve
Cynthia rosy-crimson
Earl of Donoughmore bright red
Hollandia deep pink
Kluis Triumph red
Lamplighter light red
Lavender Girl mauve
Madame de Bruin bright red
Marianus Koster pink, dark blotch
Marion Street pink
Mrs Charles Pearson pale mauve fading to white
Mrs G. W. Leak light pink, dark blotch
Old Port deep red

Percy Wiseman creamy-pink
Pink Pearl pink
Professor Hugo de Vries deep pink
Purple Splendour purple
Susan lavender

Late Flowering Rhododendrons

Species
R. auriculatum white
R. campylogynum strawberry-red
R. decorum white-flushed pink
R. diaprepes white
R. discolor pale pink to white
R. ferrugineum pink
R. griersonianum geranium-scarlet
R. lepidostylum pale yellow
R. lepidotum red-purple/deep purple
R. makinoi pink
R. ponticum mauve
R. serotinum white, purple blotch
R. triflorum light yellow

Hybrids
A. Bedford mauve, dark blotch
Baroness Schroeder white, dark blotch
Chionoides white, yellow eye
Diphole Pink pink
Frank Galsworthy dark pink, yellow blotch
Goldsworth Orange orange
Gomer Waterer white, yellow blotch
Helen Schiffner white
Kate Waterer pink, yellow blotch
Kluis Sensation scarlet-red
Lady Annette de Trafford pink dark spot
Lady Clementine Mitford pink, yellow centre
Marchioness of Lansdowne rose-pink, black spot
Michael Waterer deep red
Mrs Davies Evans mauve
Mrs T. Lowinsky white, brown blotch

Sappho white, black spot
Souvenir de D. A. Koster bright red
Spitfire dark red
Sweet Simplicity pale pink
Viscount Powerscourt red, large blotch

Good Whites

Species
R. auriculatum white
R. decorum white-flushed pink
R. falconeri creamy-white
R. serotinum white, purple blotch
R. yakushimanum pink bud fading to pure white

Hybrids
Avalanche white
Caroline de Zoete white
Cilpinense white
Cunningham's White white
Fragrantissimum white
Gomer Waterer light pink fading to pure white, yellow blotch
Hyperion white, chocolate blotch
Loderi King George pink bud fading to pure white
Mrs A. T. de la Mare white, green centre
Mrs T. H. Lowinsky white, brown blotch
Sappho white, black spot

Good Reds

Species
R. barbatum crimson-scarlet
R. campylogynum strawberry-red
R. forrestii var. repens scarlet
R. griersonianum geranium-scarlet
R. haematodes blood-red
R. thomsonii blood-red

Hybrids
Anna Rose Whitney bright red
Britannia scarlet
Earl of Athlone deep red

141

Earl of Donoughmore bright red
Elizabeth Hobbie red
Kluis Triumph red
Lamplighter light red
Old Port deep red
President Roosevelt red, white throat
Surrey Heath light red, white throat
Wilgens Ruby red

Good Blues/Purples/Lavenders/Lilacs/Mauves

Species
R. campanulatum blue-purple
R. ponticum mauve
R. russatum purple

Hybrids
Augfast blue
Blue Diamond blue
Blue Peter lavender-blue
Lavender Girl lilac
Mrs Charles Pearson pale mauve
Mrs Davies Evans mauve
Praecox mauve
Purple Splendour purple
Susan lavender

Good Pinks

Species
R. dauricum rosy-pink
R. orbiculare rosy-pink
R. racemosum deep pink
R. souliei soft rose
R. williamsianum pink

Hybrids
Chevalier Felix de Sauvage deep pink
Corona coral pink
Cynthia rosy-crimson

Diphole Pink pink
Hydon Dawn pink
Lady Clementine Mitford pink, yellow centre
Marion Street pink
Mrs Furnivall light pink, red blotch
Percy Wiseman creamy-pink
Pierre Moser pink, light centre
Pink Pearl pink
Racil blush
Tessa light pink

Good Yellows

Species
R. campylocarpum yellow
R. lepidostylum pale yellow
R. lutescens yellow
R. triflorum light yellow
R. wardii yellow

Hybrids
Curlew yellow
Diane light yellow
Fortune yellow
Goldsworth Yellow apricot-yellow
Igtham Yellow good yellow
Mrs Betty Robinson near-yellow
Princess Anne yellow
Unique creamy yellow
Yellow Hammer yellow

Rhododendrons Suitable for Container Cultivation

Plants with bushy, compact growth
Blue Peter lavender-blue
Britannia scarlet
C. B. van Nes red
R. caucasicum Pictum pale rose/pale yellow
Chevalier Felix de Sauvage deep pink

Chionoides white, yellow eye
Corona pink
Cunningham's White pink bud fading to white
Cynthia rosy-crimson
Doncaster red
Hollandia carmine
Lady Annette de Trafford pink, yellow spot
Mrs T. H. Lowinsky white, brown blotch
Souvenir de D. A. Koster bright red
Sweet Simplicity pale pink
Trilby dark red
Unique cream/yellow

Early flowerers for indoors
R. caucasicum Pictum pale rose/pale yellow
Chevalier Felix de Sauvage deep pink
Christmas Cheer pale pink
Jacksonii pink
Nobleanum cultivars
Pierre Moser pink, light centre
Praecox mauve
Prince Camille de Rohan pink, red blotch

Plants with attractive foliage
Abigail pink/orange
R. decorum white-flushed pink
R. fortunei pink to white
Furnivall's Daughter pink, dark blotch
Goldsworth Orange orange
Lady Clementine Mitford pink, yellow centre
Lady Eleanor Cathcart deep pink, dark blotch
Marion Street pink
Moser's Maroon maroon
President Roosevelt red, light blotch
R. yakushimanum hybrids

INDEX